General Ioan Emanoil Florescu
Organizer of the Romanian Army

Radu Florescu

2007
East European Monographs, Boulder, Colorado
Distributed by Columbia University Press, New York

East European Monographs, No.DCCXV

ISBN: 978-0-88033-613-0
Library of Congress Control Number: 2007935636

Printed in the United States of America

CONTENTS

FORWARD
By General Dr. Mihai E. Ionestu

General Ioan Emanoil Florescu (1819-1893) was an outstanding figure for the destiny of the modern Romanian army. More than a mere monograph was necessary to outline the will, the tenacity, and the sense of responsibility that he made proof of in his courageous and difficult work of restructuring the national military system during a decisive period of our history governed by two major events: the Union of the Principalities and the achievement of State Independence. We have it now due to the competent effort of one of the General's descendants, Professor Radu Florescu, from Boston College (U.S.A.).

Descent of ancient boyars in Wallachia, the future General came from the first generation of young men who were sent in increasingly larger numbers to the West to complete their studies with an eye to their future. Graduate of St. Louis Lyceum (1840) and of the General Staff School in Paris (1842), Ioan Emanoil Florescu acquired the necessary skills for an army career.

One should remember that the pre-conditions for the establishment of a modern military system were already in part accomplished in the second half of the 19th century. First of all because the movement for the Union of the Principalities had created a propitious environment for "the formation of a national army" according to General H. Herkt,[1] one of General Florescu's contemporaries." Because of his background and schooling General Florescu had the power to implement the reform of the military system established by Prince Alexandru Ioan Cuza and continued by Prince Carol of Hohenzollern. His appointment as head of the Ministry of War in Iasi (October 11/23, 1859) and later in Bucharest (August 30/September 11, 1860) represented the first Union of the Principalities of Moldavia and Wallachia. Florescu's experience acquired in the field of military organization under Alexandru Ioan Cuza's rule and later as Minister of War (1871-1876) served him in good stead. He completed the restructuring of the army and put into practice the reform program proposed by the future King Carol I. In essence, he prepared the Romanian army for the War for National Independence (1878-1879).

During his entire activity, the subject of the present monograph, General Ioan Emanoil Florescu proved his sense of responsibility, commitment, and will power founded both on love of country and unswerving loyalty to the idea of a national army.

Due to his distinguished scientific effort, Professor Radu R. Florescu succeeded not only in bringing his illustrious precursor to the readers'

[1] General Herkt, *Several pages from the history of our army (A Veteran's memories during his call),* Bucharest, 1902, p. 58.

attention but also in filling a void in Romanian historiography. Undoubtedly for a family member to write about the life and activities of a prominent relative is a difficult task particularly when the name has historic resonance. Such an attempt is all the more difficult when the author is emotionally involved in the subject matter and at the same time obliged to find the correct balance between personal sentiment and historical truth. Professor Florescu's scientific work is remarkable and deserves the readers' attention. We are therefore honored to publish this monograph under the aegis of the Institute for Political Studies of Defense and Military History, which consider Professor Radu Florescu among its collaborators and constant friends.

General Dr. Mihai E. Ionestu

Director of the Institute for Political Studies of Defense
and Military History

PREFACE

This book written in the spirit of the ever-lasting Franco-Romanian friendship was inspired by two brilliant military men who were war historians themselves.

The first is my uncle, Colonel Radu Miclescu, from Queen Marie's own 4th Rosiori Regiment; a student of the St. Cyr Academy and of the War College in Paris, severely injured at the Battle of Oituz during the great war in 1916, military attaché of the Romanian Legation in Paris, member of the Romanian equestrian team and decorated with the French Legion of Honor. He is the author of an original work, *Study on the National Defense* (Bucharest, 1929), in which he foresaw the importance of aviation in wars to come. In 1940 he resigned from the army as a colonel, thus protesting the Soviet Union's annexation of Bessarabia. Colonel Miclescu wrote many manuscripts concerning the Romanian army which he wasn't allowed to publish during the communist period. The author had the satisfaction to celebrate Ceausescu's downfall together with a bottle of champagne and the "rosette" of the Legion of Honor, which I had brought from France.

The second General Maurice Durosoy, a cousin of my wife Nicole, director of the French Cavalry School in Saumur, former military attaché of the French Embassy in London for many years official representative of the French government in the U.S.A. on Armistice Day. General Durosoy served in Morocco, under the command of Marshal Lyautey, whose biography he wrote: *Lyautey – mon general* a work which was regarded by the French Academy. He also wrote a history of Saumur, the former cavalry school, currently a tank school. We arranged trips for American students to visit various locations where Napoleon's greatest battles had taken place. This French-Romanian collaboration is well represented today by my son, Radu, Director of Saatchi & Saatchi Company and by his wife Helene, both of them continuing to work in the best interests of France and Romania.

Radu Florescu

Professor Emeritus
Boston College

DEDICATION AND ACKNOWLEDGEMENTS

I would like to dedicate this monograph to my uncle Gheorghe Dumitru Florescu, former Director of the Museum of Bucharest City, historian, archivist, archeologist, member of the Romanian Genealogical Association, and author of several books and articles. He specialized in the history of the boyar families of Wallachia, and the history of Bucharest. Rarely in my life have I found a scholar who would spend his time helping students and colleagues with valuable, precise and well-documented information, with no other interest other than searching the historical truth. A perfect gentleman, brought up in the good old tradition of the 19th century, wearing the outfit of that period, he specialized in the history of the Florescu family and fought hard to preserve what was left of a small family monastery built at Strejnicu Gaiseni. Married to Marga Cantacuzino, the "Nabab's" daughter – the former owner of the present Enescu museum, he had a hard life during the communist period with his four daughters and two sons. One of them, Manole is a doctor living near Bucharest.

When I met my uncle for the first time I experienced a very emotional moment. I – an American – was visiting a relative who had lost a daughter and most of his library during an American air raid over Bucharest. But when he saw that I was an historian who loves Romania, he hugged me, proud that I was the only one in the family who had embraced his career. He placed at my disposal the Florescu archives which helped me write the present monograph.

The second figure, who had great influence upon my professional career and even played a decisive part in it, was the late Professor Constantin C. Giurescu.

The third important personality to whom I owe a lifelong gratitude is Academician Cornelia Bodea with whom I collaborated in all my works.

I owe this study to an IREX American scholarship within the program of cultural exchanges in the fields of Education, Science and Technology, in 1977-1978. The research took place at the Nicolae Iorga History Institute, the University of Bucharest, the Center of Historical Studies and Research on Military Theory, and the Central Library at the Ministry of National Defense, the State Archives in Bucharest and its branch in Iasi.

My gratitude goes to all the specialists who helped me at the time. I would like to mention among them the late Christian Popisteanu, editor of *Magazin Istoric* who encouraged me to publish certain articles about General Florescu. I also want to thank General Mihail E. Ionescu, Director of the Institute for Political Studies on Defense and Military History, and Mrs. Maria Georgescu for all the support that she offered in completing this monograph, particularly for the constructive observations during the preparation of the manuscript. I owe Distinguished Professor Stephen

Fisher-Galati, Editor of the East European Quarterly and East European Monographs distributed by Columbia University Press, my first studies on General Florescu within the series of volumes *War and Society in East Central Europe* and for agreeing to publish an English translation of the original Romanian text ably prepared by Andrei Pandea, the director at the Military Printing House (Editura militara) in Bucharest. The English text was prepared by Mrs. Karen Potterton of the Boston College History Department, a friend of long date with an uncanny talent for deciphering my poor calligraphy.

Since I am not up to date on the latest techniques of the computer age, I would also like to pay tribute to Mrs. Laura Calous and Andreea Bernicu for the passion and patience shown to a professor (who changes his texts very often) for help in the preparation of this work.

I am grateful to my wife, Nicole, for the patience and understanding shown over the several months when she was deprived of my attention.

Radu Florescu

Professor Emeritus
Boston College

INTRODUCTION

General Ioan Emanoil Florescu (1817-1893) founder of the Romanian modern army is one of the few figures of the 19th century whose biography still remains in the researchers' attention. As a soldier, statesman, and educator, General Florescu was among Prince Cuza's four closest collaborators. He can be seen on the Prince's pedestal at Union Square in Iasi next to the Prince's other close collaborators Costache Negri, Mihail Kogalniceanu and Emanuel Kretulescu. In a speech delivered at the Romanian Academy in 1936, "General I. Em. Florescu – A Forgotten Figure," the military historian General Radu Rosetti clearly outlined the fact that indeed he was unfortunately forgotten.

It may seem presumptuous for a family member to write about one of his distinguished predecessors. But this idea partly occurred to me because my uncle, Gheorghe D. Florescu, had gathered numerous documents, a genuine archive about the General, many of those papers unknown to historians. Being appointed a researcher at the Fulbright Foundation in 1967, and having the opportunity to use Prince Cuza's documentary archive, assembled by historian Constantin C. Giurescu, I was encouraged by Giurescu to use the archive. Giurescu told me,"I think it's time to encourage a young historian to begin research on General Florescu's career." I don't know whether it was his encouragement or his manner of persuading me that I embarked upon this task. I would have preferred for someone else to write this biography. However, as a member of the family, it occurred to me that a monograph might urge others to complete it with a definitive biography.

A short history of the ancient Florescu Boyar family, who fought for centuries on the side of the first native princes to protect the borders of the country, would help us understand the patriotism of their descendant. It may have been destiny or perhaps their own wish to remain hidden in the shadows of history. The family belonged to the class of "Great Boyars" the first to be mentioned by surname in the 15th century, at a time when most of their kinsmen would sign the documents of the princely chancellery with their Christian names and Byzantine court titles.

The first Florescu was better known to history was Vintila who served in the Council of Vlad Tepes (also known as the Impaler (Dracula). His younger brother was known as Radu the Handsome, a friend of the Turks with the title of *clucer* (Court Victualler), and later under his successors that of *logofat* (a logothete, a high ranking boyar). The relationships between the Florescu family and the princely family of the Basarabs remain mysterious. By the end of the 18th century when Ion Budai-Deleanu wrote the first historical epic in Romanian dedicated to the memory of Vlad Tepes, the only boyar he mentioned was Florescu, a friend of the gypsies and an enemy of evil forces such as the Turks, the devils and other villains and ghosts of the Retezat Mountains. On the other hand it is also possible that Vintila's sister, Maria, who eventually became a nun and took the name of Eupraxia, may have married for the second time one of Vlad Tepes's worst enemies, the third illegitimate son of Vlad Dracul, thus Dracula's half brother. His name was Vlad Calugarul (Vlad the Monk) or Vlad the IV, and he was prince in Wallachia during 1482-1495. He was buried at the Glavacioc Monastery, near Bucharest.

A century later, another Florescu, bearing the name of Radu and perhaps the stepbrother of Mihai the Brave, became one of the most trustworthy emissaries of this prince in Constantinople. He undoubtedly helped the prince to obtain the throne of Wallachia. This candidacy became a very significant historic event because Mihai the Brave was the first prince who succeeded in reuniting the three Romanian provinces for a short period of time.

During the 1848 revolution, the Florescu household in Bucharest, located in the suburb of Scortar, just like the Golescu house, turned into one of the main revolutionary centers in the country where the revolution and the uprising itself was planned. During the Russian administration of the Organic Statute, most of the family members preferred the less depressing atmosphere of Paris, studying at the Sorbonne or College de France. Later in 1848 they fought on the barricades in Paris before taking part in the Revolution in Bucharest. When the revolution was put down by Russia they went back to Paris or elsewhere in exile. Some of them dedicated their life to study, others like Dumitru Florescu, my great-grandfather, one of the founders of the Conservatory of Music in Bucharest, compensated his disappointment by composing patriotic songs such as "Hora Unirii." Dumitru's sister, Alexandra or Luxita, the "black sheep" of the family, eloped with Nicolae Balcescu and gave him an illegitimate son, called Bonifaciu. He maintained the name of Florescu and became a teacher and a critic of French literature.

Patriotism was always a chief characteristic for all the members of the Florescu family, men or women. At the same time their personality was dominated by modesty and perseverance. A very good example is the career of my grandfather, Alexadru D. Florescu, one of the founders of the Cultural League which protected the interests of the Romanian citizens in Transylvania. He was also the General's nephew and he worked as his secretary in 1891 when the General was prime minister. Perhaps all these figures deserve a separate study in order to save them from total oblivion but General Florescu alone deserves an entire volume.

The General's life may be considered from different aspects: military, political, cultural and private. His military career comprises several distinctive stages. The first one is related to the Organic Statute, a period when he completed his education and military studies in Paris and Bucharest, under the rules of his fathers-in-law, Princes Gheorghe Bibescu and Barbu Stirbey. During the second period, possibly the most difficult, General Florescu laid the foundations of a national army under Prince Cuza, by unifying the Moldavian and the Wallachian armies; this union preceded the political union of the country. Later, as minister of war, under Prince Carol's rule, he organized a truly modern Romanian army which, in spite of its inherent needs, secured the country's national independence on the Bulgarian battlefields. The final stage of General Florescu's career comprises several offices, both political and cultural. He was twice prime minister (in 1876 and 1891), minister of internal affairs and public works (1865-1866), chairman of the senate (1882), professor at the War Academy, member of the Romanian Athenaeum (1865), chairman of the Society for Education of the Romania people and chairman of the Target Shooting, and Physical Education Association.

For this mini-biographic presentation, we shall attempt to describe the character traits of this distinguished man and outline the various stages of his fascinating career which left its mark on the entire period and is clearly linked to the beginnings of the modern Romanian army.

CHAPTER 1

THE EVOLUTION OF THE ROMANIAN ARMY UNTIL THE UNION OF THE PRINCIPALITIES OF MOLDAVIA AND WALLACHIA

Following the foundation of the Principalities, in the 13th and 15th centuries, the princes of the Romanian provinces, Wallachia and Moldavia, had always had an army – the "people-in-arms" – comprising a "small army" and a "large army."[1] The "small army" was made up of boyars and their suites and was represented by cavalry units well protected with armor, swords and short spears, comparable with Western feudal armies. On the other hand, the "large army" was a very original force which cannot be found in neighboring countries. It consisted of free peasants – *mosneni* in Wallachia and *razesi* in Moldavia, equipped with bows and arrows who were called to arms only in times of danger. This force offered the princes the possibility of assembling up to 40,000-50,000 men, quite an impressive number for two small countries having less than one million inhabitants. The princes also had at their disposal their personal guard – the courtiers – a sort of a police unit which protected the fortifications on the border often placed in small castles in the mountain areas. The boyar in command after the prince at the helm of the armed forces was the Spathar in Wallachia and the Hatman in Moldavia. Because of rivalries for the princely throne within the Basarab family the partisans of Prince Dan (known as The Danestis) and those of Dracula (The Draculestis) provide a good example. Divisons also occurred among the upper Boyar families. The "large army" became very important during the Dracula period. As the *calarasi* (and *voinici* in Moldavia) started to replace "unworthy" boyars, a new infantry was created (the *archers*, the *sagetori* and the *dorobanti).* As early as the 15th century there was even a sort of artillery which comprised imprecise "bombards," primitive cannons with stone or iron projectiles used during the siege of the Danubian port-cities occupied by the Turks.

Steven the Great (1457-1504), prince in Moldavia, could mobilize an army of up to 60,000 men, most of them on horseback which also comprised a personal guard of 3,000 courtiers and mercenaries who in time of victory would share in the loot captured from the enemy. Church bells would toll calling men to the arms while mobilization took place under the command of a *parcalab,* the "governors of well-known fortresses." These castles were protected by powerful walls, barricades and donjons. Michael the Braves's (1593-1601) armies were less numerous than Steven the Great's – 12,000 men at the battle of Calugareni. They consisted of boyar

[1]Calin Hentea, Armata si luptele romanilor. Breviar de istorie, Bucharest, 2002, page 98.

families faithful to the prince to the end, such as the Craiovescus, the Buzescus, the Calomfirescus and Florescus; the princely guards and the courtiers were often identified as "country reds" judging by the red cloth which they obtained at Christmas and Easter.[2] Michael the Brave, the first prince to achieve the Union of the three Principalities, was forced just like Steven the Great, to call to arms not only the peasantry but also foreign mercenaries who eventually betrayed him. Although Michael had few gunners he preferred side arms, his personal courage and the use of the latest tactics and military strategies enabled us to consider him among one of the great war captains of all times. Although far removed from the glory attained in previous centuries, Michael the Brave's successors, for a time preserved almost intact the army's basic organizational structure the "calarasi," the "country reds," the "darabani" (later called "dorobanti,") the foreign mercenaries, volunteers from the south of the Danube, as well as Poles, Ukrainians and Cossacks from the north of Moldavia.[3] All these military units: the infantry, the cavalry, an artillery, a flotilla on the Danube comprised the Principalities' army. In addition barracks were built for the soldiers, military music had its role in war and there were distinctive flags and insignias for each principality, all survivals of the past.

After the Ottomans appointed the Greek princes of the Phanar (meaning the lighthouse section of Constantinople) during the 18th century in order to punish the last autonomous Romanian princes such as Dimitrie Cantemir and Constantin Brancoveanu who had betrayed the sultan, it became obvious that both countries had lost their interest in maintaining traditional armies. The Phanariot Princes kept a personal guard made up of Greek, Albanian and Serbian mercenaries, essentially bodyguards. The boyars, their sons and even the free peasants began to look for work in the armies of neighboring counties, such as the Habsburg Empire and Tsarist Russia. As a result of the many occupations by those two empires during the 18th century, many Romanians were enthused by the Napoleonic epic in Eastern Europe, all the more so since France was a "Latin sister." Napoleon himself was seen as a liberator of the Orient, at least in words.

During the Phanariot regime outlawry started to spread against the Greek princes, and their newly appointed boyars and other rich exploiters. We may say that by the end of the 18th century there was no national army in Wallachia or Moldavia besides the mercenary guards. In Moldavia, Russia's neighbor, the principal force belonged to the Russian command, which considered this principality as belonging to them. However, a revolutionary movement occurred in Wallachia in 1821 consisting of a force of 12,000 free peasants, "panduri," and a handful of boyar cavalry

---

[2]Before Mihai Viteazul, Matei Basarab used to call "country reds" the permanent cavalry.
[3]Nicolae Stoicescu, L'armee de la Valachie sous regne de Michel le Brave (1593-1601), in "Revue des Etudes Sud-Est Europeenes," vol. XXIII, 1975, no. 3.

(2,000) – "the people's assembly."[4] They were under the command of a small boyar, Tudor of Vladimir, who had acquired his military experience as a volunteer in the Russian army, during the Russo-Turkish war (1806-1812). He had both social and national goals, but the money came from the leaders of a Greek society "Philike Hetaeria," established by Prince Alexandre Ypsilanti at Odessa. The movement was condemned by tsar Alexander I a fact which convinced Alexandru Ypsilanti to sentence Tudor Vladimirescu to death, as a traitor of the Greek revolutionary movement.

The most important consequence of Tudor Vladimirescu's death was the Turks' decision to bring back native princes in the Romanian Principalities when they understood that the Phanariots had in turn betrayed the interests of the Ottoman Empire.

This short period of autonomy which followed the Phanariot regime was interrupted by the Russo-Turkish war (1828-1829) which ended with the conclusion of Treaty of Adrianople.

Beside its negative aspects, such as the temporary occupation of the Romanian Principalities by Russia and the imposition of tsarist protectorate, the treaty also had a positive side which was very significant for the Principalities; it concerned their political status *vis a vis* the Ottoman Empire as well as their internal administration.[5] It restated and consolidated the autonomy of the Romanian Principalities towards Turkey and at the same time authorized Russia to issue a fundamental law concerning the internal organization of the two provinces (also known as the Organic Statute) or (Reglement Organique).

The regulations were drafted at Saint Petersburg, by a Russo-Romanian commission led by Pavel Kiseleff, the only Russian general whose departure was truly regretted by the Romanians. The Regulations were voted in Wallachia in 1831 and in Moldavia in 1832. This law concerning the internal organization laid the foundation of similar modern administrative institutions for each province which hastened the process of the union of the two Principalities. One of the goals of this strategy was the formation of two national armies, called "militia" in Wallachia and the "land guard" in Moldavia. However, the idea of founding a people's army

---

[4]Radu R. Florescu, The Struggle against Russia in the Danubian Principalities, The Romanian Academic Association, Munich, 1983, page 84; also see: Andrei Otetea, Tudor Vladimirescu si revolutia din 1821, Bucharest, 1971; Dan Berindei, L'annee revolutionnaire 1821 dans les Pays Roumains, Bucharest, 1973; Gheorghe Iscru, Prelegeri de istorie moderna. Revolutia din 1821 condusa de Tudor Vladimirescu, Bucharest, 1975; Mircea T. Radu, Tudor Vladimirescu si Revolutia din 1821 din Tara Romaneasca, Craiova, 1978.

[5]Acte si documente relative la Istoria Renasterii Romaniei, Bucharest, 1888, col. I, pages 318-325; Istoria Romaniei, Vol. III, Bucharest, 1964, pages 927-931. Colectia vechilor legiuiri administrative. Regulamentele organice ale Valahiei si Moldovei, Bucharest, 1894, pages 183-201, 450-452; D. Ionescu, C. Tutui, Gh. Matei, Dezvoltarea constitutionala a statului roman, Bucharest 1957, pages 74-75

under separate command survived as a leitmotif during all the great moments in Romanians history such as the epic of Mihai the Brave, the Revolution of Tudor Vladimirescu and the 1848 revolutionary movement. "*Without the appropriate weapons we shall not be able to save our country from the hands of those who have robbed it during all these years*" stated Tudor Vladimirescu in 1821.[6]

Nicolae Balcescu, the well known revolutionary figure began his studies of Romanian history with a book entitled *The Armed Power and the Military Art from the Foundation of the Wallachian Principality up to Now* (1844), followed by *The Armed Power and the Military Art of the Moldavians during their Greatness* (1846). He saw the army as an institution called upon to support the national program. It is by no mere coincidence that the work which crowns his activity in the field of historiography is entitled: *The Romanian under Prince Michael the Brave* perhaps the most significant moment in the struggle led by the Romanian people's ancestors for national unity.[7]

The appearance of the first military uniforms in Bucharest and in Iasi, designed "Russian style," generated enthusiastic reactions from the inhabitants of the two cities. *Albina Romaneasca*, the Iasi newspaper, wrote at the time: "Every Romanian seems to see his nation born once again." "The young people coming from all over the country and belonging to all the social classes rushed to enroll under the flags of the new organizations," added Dimitrie Papazoglu, "a Junker" in the Wallachian army.[8]

The main idea of the Organic Statutes concerning the army was based on article 5 of the Adrianople Convention, which laid the foundations of the two Romanian armies that had not existed during the Phanariot period. "*The governments of the two principalities have the liberty to establish sanitary stations along the Danube and elsewhere inside the country.... Each principality will support a very strict number of guards to man the quarantine station to watch over the security of the borders, to preserve order in cities and villages, and respect laws and regulations. The number and upkeep of these militias [sic!] will be decided by the hospodars together with the divans, according to previous customs.*"[9]

"The national militia," established in 1831 according to the *Army Regulations concerning the local militia of the Wallachian Principality* and the *Regulations concerning local guard of the Moldavian Principality* comprised a permanent army aiming at identical administrative tasks,

[6]George Ioan Lahovary, Hartii vechi. Geneza ostirii romanesti, 1830, Bucharest, 1893, page 8; Albina romaneasca, year II, no. 48, June 26, 1830, page 201.
[7]Valeriu Stan, Nicolae Balcescu, 1819-1852, Bucharest, 1977, pages 27; 81-83.
[8]Albina romaneasca, year II, no. 48, June 26, 1830, page 201.
[9]V. Nadejde, Centenarul renasterii armatei romane (1830-1930), Iasi, 1930, page 27 or 58. Regarding the army's organization of the two Principalities, also see Major I. Popovici, Organizarea armatei romane, Vol. I, Roman, 1900; General Ion I. Anastasiu, Oastea romanilor de-a lungul veacurilor, Bucharest, 1933.

namely that of preserving order, securing the country's frontiers, control the sanitary installations established by the Russians (quarantine stations), to ward off plague epidemics, guard the customs and salt mines, and collect taxes in cities and villages.

In the course of time subtle changes occurred encouraged by the Princes of the Reglement period even though they were *de facto* under the control of the Russian pro-consuls. Thus, Princes Alexandru Ghica (1834-1842), Gheorghe Bibescu (1842-1848), Barbu Stirbey (1849-53) in Wallachia and Mihai Sturdza (1834-1849), and Grigore Ghica (1854-56) in Moldavia tried to secretly militarize many of the provisions regarding the organization, training, number of recruits and strategic goals inherent in the original document. For instance the number of the non-permanent territorials: dorobanti, cordonasi and potecasi in Wallachia and the slujitori and plaiesi in Moldavia were often assigned "military" rather than "police" functions even though they continued to be essentially concerned with the administrative obligations. This enabled the permanent troops to focus on military duties in the strict sense.

In this manner small infantry and cavalry units were formed called national militia in Wallachia (4700 men) and "land guards" in Moldavia (1554 men). These permanent troops were recruited by lot in villages; one man for 70 families to serve for a six year period following which they were exempt from military service. The officers were appointed by the Prince from the Boyar class with the title of "Junker" in Wallachia and "cadet" in Moldavia. The budget was to be submitted to the Parliamentary Assembly for a six-year period. The morale of this new small army was none of the best since many recruits felt abandoned by their families during their period of service.

Thus, in spite of the many interdictions of the protecting powers particularly the watchful eyes of the Russian pro consuls an embryo of two national armies began to take shape with native princes attempting to undermine Russia's ostensible leading authority. For instance, it was Prince Alexander Ghica of Wallachia who founded a Princely General Staff (Stabul Domnesc) which later became the Army Administration. By 1849 an Army Council functioned by the Prince's side. It was only following Russia's defeat in the Crimean war in 1856 that the army administration took the name of Army Department which in certain princely documents was also known as the Ministry of War.

In terms of the progress of the army during the Reglement period the artillery was founded as a separate unit which comprised of three canons given by the Turks on the occasion of Prince George Bibescu's visit to Constantinople in 1842. A small flotilla composed of three gunboats was also anchored on the Danube. The first army barracks, an armory, a munitions factory, powder mills, a small sanitary unit, judiciary and administrative departments, workshops and army stores were built during the period. Officer training also began. The Russians whose interest was to maintain a small submissive army invariably preferred sending Boyar trainees to complete their studies at military academies at St. Petersburg or at least Berlin. Since sending young Boyars to the West was a difficult option at the time the Princes initially attempted to teach tactics and strategy in spite of Russian opposition. In 1847 the establishment of an officer's school in Bucharest laid the foundation of an autonomous military education though the courses were interrupted by the 1848 revolution. They were to be resumed only in 1850. It was in 1856 after the Crimean war that a provisional Regimental school later to be called the Military School was founded in Iassy.[10]

More ambitious than the nationalized military establishment was the reawakening of the traditional ideal of the "the nation in arms" an appeal to all able bodied to train beside the permanent and impermanent territorial armies to defend the fatherland. In 1838 Ion Campineanu the leader of the national party favored the creation of a National Guard where every Romanian able to bear weapons should serve. The organization of a National Guard was also mentioned in the program of the revolutionaries of 1848 essentially an appeal to the peasantry.

In spite of all these improvements the Reglement armies in both Principalities were not really capable of initiating serious military operations because they had no training for that purpose. A good example was the heroic resistance of the Bucharest firemen who were only somewhat militarized. Though they fought courageously against the Turkish army which had been sent to quell the revolutionaries of 1848 at Dealul Spirei in Bucharest, the firemen were eventually defeated by a superior force.[11] In Moldavia there was no resistance when the Russians intervened. Both Turks and Russians reimposed the reactionary governments of the Reglement Period while the leaders of the revolution fled in exile or were imprisoned.

As already noted the defeat of Russia by the Anglo-French and Sardinian forces played a very important part in the further development of the armies of Moldavia and Wallachia. Article 27 of the Treaty of Paris which terminated the War specified that the Russian Protectorate over the Principalities initially established in 1829 was terminated and that the southern portion of Bessarabia which had been annexed by the czar would be returned to Moldavia. In securing the new frontiers it was further specified (Article 42) that the militias of both Principalities would be

---

[10]Cornelia Bodea, Lupta romanilor pentru unitate nationala (1834-1849), Bucharest, 1967, page 222.

[11]Constantin Cazanisteanu, Probleme militare in "Revolutia de la 1848," in Revolutia de la 1848 in Tarile Romane, pages 131-143. Also see Radu R. Florescu, The Struggle against Russia in the Danubian Principalities, The Romanian Academic Association, Munich, 1983, page 223.

organized in a similar manner and eventually "form a single army" if needed. From this point on many young Romanian officers in both Principalities would be able to attend French or other western military schools to complete their military education.

The formidable task of transforming the armies of Moldavia and Wallachia into a single military force was given to one of the few soldiers who had the advantage of having been trained within the old framework of the Russian sponsored Reglement organization. However, he had the additional advantage of French military schooling, by far the best at that period. His name was Colonel Ion Emanoil Florescu who also had the good fortune of having befriended the soon to be elected Prince of the Moldo-Wallachian state, Alexander Ion Cuza.

CHAPTER II

THE YOUTH AND EDUCATION OF IOAN EMANOIL FLORESCU

General I. E. Florescu was born on August 7, 1819, at Vizuresti in the district of Ramnicu-Valcea. The date of his birth was found on a copy bearing genealogical notes belonging to George D. Florescu, a former Director of the Museum of the city of Bucharest. The copy was made according to a manuscript with psalms in Greek belonging to Ionita Florescu, a former great vornic (governor) (1742-1801) and the father of Manolache Florescu. Ioan Emanoil was his son. Though it had been in the possession of the General himself, the manuscript was lost as a result of repeated legacies to other members of the family, among which his daughter Ecaterina Ghica and her sister, Baroness Maria Szent-Kereszty.

Ioan Emanoil's parents were Manolache Florescu and Zinca Faca. In time they moved to Bucharest, in the suburb of Saint Spiridon, during their son's studies.[1] The boy's name is mentioned in 1832 in the registers of the "St. Sava" National College, well known at the time for its progressive faculty and the quality of its students, future reformers of the Romanian society, such as Nicolae Balcescu[1] In 1832-1833, young Florescu was among the graduates of St. Sava College who excelled in Mathematics and Science which the future military man was going to master to perfection. On the other hand, the young student did not neglect the study of literature and he tried his skills as an actor in Romanian and French plays; he also distinguished himself by his translations in French, a language which he spoke fluently even from the first schooling years.

In 1833 just like many other young men of his time, Florescu, aged 14, with the rank of "Junker" reserved only for sons of boyars enthusiastically enrolled in the new army, which was formed in 1830-1831 as we have already seen. When he returned to Bucharest on holiday in 1834-35, his grandmother Alexandrina, the sister of Prince Alexandru Ghica (1834-1842), found the young soldier on guard in mid-winter at the Princely palace where there was a reception.[2] She got permission from the Prince to invite her grandson to the palace ball, while the "Junker" Petrache Romanescu took over his duties at the palace gate. Among other debutantes, Florescu more than likely met the daughter of the future prince Gheorghe Bibescu soon to be elected in 1842 in competition with Florescu's father and his uncle who were themselves candidates to the throne.

At the age of 16, Florescu was sent to Paris by Alexander Ghica with the rank of "parucic" (officer cadet), in spite of the instructions which had come from St. Petersburg, where the regime afraid of French influence

[1]Valeriu Stan, *Nicolae Balcescu*, page 20.

[2]Regarding the Ghica family, see M. D. Sturdza, *Grandes familles de Grèce, D'Albanie et de Constantinople*, Paris, 1983, pages 297-299.

preferred to send talented soldiers to the capital of Russia for study, or, failing that to Berlin. In Paris, Florescu was among the first Romanian students who spent four years at Saint Louis le Grand Lyceum and two more years at the prestigious General Staff School for military training (1840-1842).[3] During his years in France he enrolled in the 2nd Infantry Regiment and he was promoted to the rank of lieutenant on April 1, 1838. He returned in the country with this rank in 1842, the year when his protector, Prince Alexandru Ghica was removed from the throne. At the age of 23, Lieutenant Florescu was undoubtedly one of the best trained soldiers in Wallachia.

Very impressed by all aspects of change in Romanian life and triggered by the ideas of certain men of culture of his time, Florescu tried to combine progressive intellectual activities with his military obligations. However, he never embraced the position of his radical comrades, the future forty-eighters, because of his nature and political convictions. This is clearly emphasized in a letter written by Dumitru Bratianu, a liberal student in Paris to his brother, Ion, asking him not to confide in Florescu, suspicious as he was of his conservatism.[4]

During his studies in the country and abroad, Ioan Emanoil, a determined nationalist who favored a moderate current of reform, turned to culture. He founded a scientific society which would promote his nationalist ideas. His chief interest however was literature. In August 1834 he and his colleagues produced a progressive play written by Florian entitled, *The Twins of Bergam*. He was to become a member of the Romanian Literary Association in 1845. His grandmother, Alexandrina Ghica, continued to watch her grandson's career even after her husband lost the throne. In 1842 she gave her grandson a mansion on Mogosoaia Bridge (today Calea Victoriei), a place which he used for his cultural activities. He lived there until 1850, when he moved to the Batiste suburb.[5] Beside his cultural activities, Florescu was very much interested in continuing his military career. That was the time when he began to be involved in training and instruction of young Junkers. He was particularly anxious to deepen their

---

[3]General Radu Rosetti, *Un uitat: Generalul Ioan Emanoil Florescu*, in "Analele Academiei Române," Mem sectunii Istorice, 3rd series, an XIX, (1937).

[4]Ionel Batalli, *Generalul Ioan Emanoil Florescu-un precursor al armatei romaine*, in Studii si Materiale Muzeografice si Istorie militara," Cental Military Museum, vol. IX, (1976), page 75.

[5]Radu Rosetti, Un uitat…, page 3: He lived in the house that his grandmother gave him in August 1842. It was on Mogosoaia Bridge, today Calea Victoriei, and it was sold by the General on March 3, 1850 when he moved to another place in Batiste suburb until he built a house on Stirbey Voda Street where he lived until 1882.

military instruction by making available to them some of the books of his military instructors in France. Among them was General Jacques Aupick,[6] Director of the General Staff School whose courses he attended and those of Captain J. Rocquancourt (*Cours élementaire d`art et d`histoire militaire à l`usage des élèves de l` école royale spéciale militaire*, vol. I-IV, 1834-1838). Florescu's translation, *The Soldier's Duties*, was in fact an elementary abstract of this book.[7]

It represented nevertheless one of the first translations in Romanian of a well-known military textbook. The General himself republished it several times.

"*I only wish that our officers as well as all the applicants for an officer rank should read it carefully.*" In 1845 he published another treatise for the use of young soldiers, *The Theory of Target Practice*, where he showed the importance of fire arms for the infantry: "*although the bayonet is very much used in wars, it is proved today that the power of an infantry lies mostly in the rapidity of its fire power.*"[8] This theory, borrowed from the new French strategy initiated by the commanding officers of Napoleon the III emphasized the importance of firearms. Florescu gave a good definition of the trajectory, followed by a bullet from the moment it leaves the barrel until it reaches its target.

Not only as a representative of the high ranking boyars and related to the famous families of the time, but mostly because of his military merit, in 1847, at the age of 26, Florescu is appointed member of the commission in charge of the formation of an officers' school. He took the task of teaching strategy and military tactics very seriously. The 1846 State Almanac refers to him as aide to Prince Gheorghe Bibescu, the successor of Alexander Ghica on the throne. In this capacity he accompanied the Prince on his journey to Constantinople in 1843, when Bibescu was inaugurated prince by the Sultan (August-September). On that occasion Florescu was pleased to bring in the country three cannons offered by the Sultan to the Romanian army. These cannons marked the beginnings of a Romanian artillery. Another factor which strengthened the bond between Bibescu and Florescu was the marriage of the young man to the Prince's daughter, Ecaterina, which took place at the Princely Palace two years after returning

---

[6]General Jacques Aupick was born in 1789; he took part in the Napoleonic wars and he was severely injured during the battle of Ligny. When he reenlisted in the army he took part in the Franco-Spanish war in 1823. He also fought in Algeria in 1834 and closed his career as the Ambassador of France in Constantinople and London.

[7]*Datoriile ostasului*, Bucharest, Socecu, Sandor and Teclu Printing House, 1876.

[8]*Teoria darii la semn*, Bucharest, Carcalechi Printing House, 1845.

to the country in 1845. Florescu was commissioned major two years after the marriage in 1847.[9]

Florescu cared deeply about his role as an army educator, a permanent trait in his entire life. It was obvious that Prince Bibescu was looking for "wise people, different from the passionate revolutionaries." In other words, soldiers who were prepared to obey orders even if they were not sympathizers of the Russian Protectorate. These were thoughts expressed by Col. Lacusteanu in his Memoirs referring to Florescu.[10]

With his French military experience Florescu was among the few officers who could be included in this category. However, contrary to what some of his opponents claimed, he was far from being a Russophile. When he was commissioned colonel and governor of prisons a few months before the beginning of the 1848 Revolution,[11] Florescu found himself in an extremely difficult position: he was a nationalist-progressive, educated in the elite French schools, but at the same time was related to Prince Bibescu and was bound to him by an oath of allegiance which he could not break. He was aware that the very members of his family who had returned from France were planning the Wallachian revolution in the Florescu family homestead in a suburb of Bucharest. At first Florescu called on the army and the police who had remained in Bucharest and asked the Russian

---

[9]Regarding Florescu's promotion under the rules of princes Bibescu and Stirbey, see *Arhiva Statului, Documente muntene*, package 103. During his marriage to Ecaterina, Bibescu's daughter he had several children: Gheorghe (January 1, 1848-January 9, 1872), Zoe (October 12, 1858-July 29, 1863), Maria (May 25, 1853-August 1891, married to Baron Szent-Kereszty), Ecaterina (November 20/December 2, 1858-July 6, 1938, married to Emanoil Ghika Brigadier General). When Ecaterina died he married Princess Alina Stirbey. They did not have any children together. The General also had an illegitimate son, Ion Constantin Grigore, born in Vienna on September 14/26, 1879 out of his affair with Iulia Viisoreanu of Turnu Severin: the child was legitimized in a letter in which he entrusted him to the care of the Florescu family. Whatever the version, the legitimization helped young Ion Constantin very much in his military career where he was commissioned to the rank of second division general. His contemporaries used to call him the "Horse" either because of his thin look or his passions for horses. On February 6, 1910 he married Elena Kalienderu who gave him two boys: Mircea Ioan (1912-1929) who died in a car accident and Ion (born in 1913), a magistrate who married Brazilian woman Countess Daisy Werther in 1934.

[10]Radu Crutescu, *Amintirile Colonelului Lacusteanu*, Bucharest, 1935, pages 232-233.

[11]Florescu's opponents claimed that when he was a governor of the prisons he used prisoners to build a house in Bucharest.

General Duhamel to head a commission to punish the officers who had broken their oath of allegiance. However, when the revolutionary government was formed and the Russian troops withdrew, Florescu was discharged from the Wallachian army. In order to extract himself from an extremely difficult situation, the former colonel decided to join the Russian army where he preserved his colonel rank and worked as an aide at the headquarters of the Russian General Luders. He justified this difficult decision on the grounds that the Hungarian revolutionaries under the leadership of Kossuth ignored the rights of the Romanian peasantry of Transylvania. Moreover the Tsarist armies had made an alliance with the Romanian leader Avram Iancu who justified his own collaboration with the Austrian and Russian forces on the grounds of Hungarian intolerance of the subject nationalities of Transylvania.[12]

The situation became much more difficult after the collapse of the Hungarian revolution and that of the Romanian forty-eighters, the leaders of which were arrested or fled into exile--including most of the members of Florescu's family. The Russians asked Barbu Stirbey Prince Bibescu's stepbrother to take over the throne under the terms of the Russian Organic Statute - establishing a regime more repressive than it was before.[13] Given Florescu's services to Russia - for which he was decorated by General Luders - it was natural for the new Prince to reintegrate Florescu in the Wallachian army and appoint him to all the offices he had held before the revolution: Princely Aide, Governor of the Prisons, to which was added the post of Minister of Communications. He continued to direct the military school where he had taught before the revolution.

On the eve of the Crimean War the situation changed once again. A Russian invasion of the Principalities in 1853 was followed by an Austrian occupation which lasted throughout the new conflict. Colonel Florescu resigned his commission for the second time and continued his career wearing a Russian uniform on a much more dangerous and important field, namely, the Crimean War. Florescu's motivation in this instance was even more difficult to understand at a time when most of his colleagues wished to volunteer in the French armies fighting the Russians. However, it could be said that his participation in that conflict at the headquarters of the Russia Generals Luders and Dannenberg represented an opportunity of putting into practice the war theories and instructions he had acquired in France. In actual fact his war activities in a major conflict in a sense completed his military training.

During the Crimean War the Russian defense consisted in reinforcing certain imposing fortifications, especially in Sevastopol, built by

---

[12]Order of the Russian Headquarters no. 77, April 30, 1850; Rosetti, op. cit. Pages 8-9.

[13]Nicolae Iorga, *Viata si Domnia lui Barbu Stirbei*, Bucharest, 1904

colonel-engineer Todleben who took the credit for this action. In this manner Florescu learned the lesson concerning the importance of the defense fortifications which represented the topic of a treatise which he published later. The great losses of the allies in open battles, such as the attack of the English cavalry at Balaklava as well as the great number of casualties caused by disease led to the organization of The Red Cross Service by Florence Nightingale.[14] The latter episode which Florescu took to heart represented a significant lesson for the future establishment of an ambulance service in Romania. Certainly the activity on a battlefield of such a great importance completed the military formation of General Florescu who was decorated for a second time by Tsar Nicholas II.

The victory of the Western powers, followed by the Congress in Paris, marked the final end of the Russian protectorate period and points to the beginning of negotiations concerning the future of the Romanian Principalities on their way to the Union. Articles 23-27 recommended the formation of a Commission to reorganize the Principalities under the protection of the victorious powers. France, Prussia, Sardinia and even Russia favored a Union, while England, and the Habsburg and Ottoman Empires were against it.

The peace concluded at Paris faced the Romanian army with another reality which affected the conscience of a new type of military man now freed from the so called protective hand of Russia. Colonel Florescu understood this reality completely and chose to resign from the Russian army shortly thereafter. He now became more concerned with the debates which followed the ad hoc divans and the elective assemblies.

On the eve of the election of Alexandru Ioan Cuza as prince of the United Principalities, Florescu resumed his role of a politician for a short time, and he abandoned the military uniform. The great powers, except for Emperor Napoleon III who had been won over to the idea of uniting Moldavia and Wallachia, thought of a temporary solution: two Principalities, two separate princes under the protection of the great powers. The ad hoc divans were to prepare the elections for the two separate assemblies which should elect the new princes. When the first non-representative and anti-unionist elections were annulled, two ad hoc divans were summoned, one for Moldavia and the other one for Wallachia where the old boyar parties fought each other. While the radical-nationalist forces supported the union of the principalities, most of the conservative boyars favored re-establishing two separate principalities, with a similar structure as in the past, when every great boyar dreamt of becoming a prince. In

[14]Florence Nightingale (1820-1910), who was the Director of a hospital in London, was sent in the Crimea in 1854 where she took care of the wounded together with 40 other English ladies. Her action contributed to the foundation of the International Red Cross.

Moldavia, the conservative boyars (the Sturdzas) represented a strong faction. But the nationalist party, although in the minority, led by Mihail Kogalniceanu, Costache Negri and Vasile Alecsandri, managed to convince the Assembly to elect Alexandru Ioan Cuza, a small boyar hailing from an old family, a man who had distinguished himself in the 1848 Revolution, was appointed governor of Galati and commander of the Moldavian troops when he returned to the country following his exile.

In Wallachia the situation was more complicated. The great boyars were divided between the partisans of the former princes Bibescu and Stirbey. Some said that Florescu himself would have been prepared to be nominated a candidate. Still this hypothesis was unlikely since at the beginning of the elections Florescu was working for his own father-in-law, Bibescu, a fact clearly outlined in his correspondence with the former prince. Eventually, on the night of January 23-24, 1859, the members of the Conservative Party who gathered in Florescu's house voted for two candidates, the vote between them being almost equally divided, Prince Bibescu and Prince Stirbey. Florescu voted for Bibescu. On the other hand the majority of the Nationalist Party in Wallachia supported the candidature of Nicolae Golescu, but he did not get a majority. When the news of Cuza's election in Moldavia became known in Bucharest it seems that General Florescu--who had had no reason to vote for him, considering Cuza's revolutionary past-changed his mind thinking about the welfare of the country and knowing that Cuza was also a military man. He then tried to persuade the conservative boyars to vote for the candidate the Moldavians had already approved, namely, Prince Cuza. According to the historian Gheorghe Florescu, the election of colonel Alexandru Ioan Cuza in Wallachia apparently took place in the very house of Ioan Emanoil Florescu in Bucharest.[15] This event was also recounted by the correspondent of "Steaua Dunarii" newspaper in Bucharest. Confirming Florescu's role in this election is the fact that Ion C. Bratianu, a member of the Nationalist Party and the enemy of Florescu, went to embrace him. Apparently the Romanian army was confined to the barracks during the election of Cuza, by order of I. C. Bratianu.

The Romanian people enthusiastically celebrated the event of the double election which represented de facto the Union of the two Principalities and the foundation of a national state. Enthusiastic meeting were held uninterruptedly in cities and villages. The army, in turn, celebrated the event; as soldiers mingled with the crowd, leading their horses by the bridle singing Hora Unirii (The Hora of Unity). General Henryk Herckt, an eye-witness to Cuza's election, said: "*Never in my career have I witnessed such solemn moments; this double election assured*

---

[15]From Gheorghe D. Florescu's archives.

the development of a national army and stimulated everybody's ideal raising the standard of that army to that of the best armies in Europe.[16]

Colonel Ioan Emanoil Florescu gave his wholehearted support to the new prince in his attempt to reorganize the army on modern lines. Ion C. Bratianu himself, described the General in a very positive manner, even though he later became his political enemy. Besides his exceptional physical qualities, Bratianu noticed Florescu's great talent in the field of military organization: "*he was the most gifted young man, with the most charming manners, with a facility to understand and even to comprehend ideas which might have been difficult for other people.*"[17] The Austrian Count Alphons von Wimpffen who had had the opportunity to know Wallachia during the occupation of 1854-1856, considered him: "*a very experienced, dynamic, and hard-working man, fair in his personal life and representing the best intelligence in the country.*"[18]

Consequently it was natural that Florescu a man of integrity and honor, passionate about the military career, endowed with initiative and humor, emotionally bonded to the soldiers under his command should unconditionally join Prince Cuza. He worked hard and selflessly to create that "steel sword" for Romania, to help secure the country's national independence. His friend Vasile Alecsandri, also one of Cuza's intimates, highlighted this trait in a poem dated following the War of Independence (January 4, 1877):

"Because every Romanian knows and feels inside
That the ancestors' sword received with you more light
And when you watch the flag with your eyes amazed
The living colors quiver in a majestic wave."[19]

---

[16]Nadejde, *Centenarul renasterii..*, Iasi, 1830, page 27. Also see General Herkt, Several pages from the history of our army (*A Veteran's Memories During His Call*), Bucharest 1902, p. 58.
[17]*Generalul Ioan Emanoil Florescu (1819-1893),* Bucharest, pages 8-9.
[18]The Austrian Count Alphons von Wimpffen had been in Wallachia during the Austrian occupation of 1854-1856. See Rosetti, quoted work, page 9.
[19]Vasile Alecsandri, *Epistola Generalului Florescu*, see appendix.

CHAPTER III

THE ORGANIZATION AND ENDOWMENT OF THE ROMANIAN ARMY UNDER ALEXANDRU IOAN CUZA'S RULE: THE GENERAL'S CONTRIBUTION

The endowment and training of the army according to modern principles commanded full attention of Prince Alexandru Ioan Cuza. The strengthening of the military was considered a task of a great importance, as important as the struggle for national entity. "*Those nations unable to fight for the preservation of their rights have disappeared.*"[1] This sentence appeared in the first issue of "*Romania militara*," a review which appeared during Cuza's rule. Nonetheless, the foremost desire of the entire nation at the time was to secure national independence. On April 25, 1859, Prince Cuza who was in Bucharest wrote to Vasile Alecsandri, Minister of External Affairs of Moldavia who was on a mission in Paris: "as a Romanian I feel the urge to uplift my country's pride in the eyes of other nations; as a Prince I am convinced of the necessity of acting in a determined manner and explore the events which are to follow...."[2]

A series of publications with suggestive titles were published during the 1860-1862 period. One of them was entitled, "*The Independence*" described as "a political, commercial and literary periodical;" another one was even a more specific "*Romanian Independence*, (1862-1863). Under the circumstances it was not surprising that people of "heart, intelligence, ability, activity, honor and patriotism" should gather around the Prince in order to tackle the expected changes in the political, economical, social and military field.[3] One of the Prince's most steady collaborators in military matters was General Ioan Emanoil Florescu who offered him unconditional support in initiating and personally supervising the great transformations which were about to come in the organization of the army. According to the Order of the Day (No. 164) issued in Bucharest on October 11, 1859, when Prince Cuza took over active command of the entire army, he specified (Order of the Day No. 243 of 1860) that "every time we shall be absent from our capital Bucharest, we authorize General Ioan E. Florescu, Minister of War to take over the active command of the troops in Wallachia."[4]

---

[1]Maria Radovici, Pagini din istoricul publicatilor militare, 1859-1910, in "Studii si materiale," Central Military Museum, no. 2-3, 1969-1970, pages 146-154.

[2]Constantin C. Giurescu, Unirea principatelor, prolog al Independentei, in "Independenta Romaniei," Bucharest, 1977, page 102. Also see R. V. Bossy, Agentia diplomatica a Romaniei la Paris si legaturile politice franco-romane sub Cuza Voda, Bucharest, 1931, pages 331-332.

[3]Nerva Hodos, Al. Sadi-Ionescu Publicatile periodicals romanesti, vol. I, Bucharest, 1913, pages 331-332.

[4]Monitorul Oastei [M.O.] (Official newspaper of the United Principalities), year I, (1860), no. 51 (December 18), page 901.

Pending state unity between Moldavia and Wallachia not to ruffle sentiments Prince Cuza proceeded with much tact and diplomacy in uniting both armies under a single War Ministry. Initially Colonel Florescu, a Wallachian, was appointed Minister of War for Moldavia while Colonel Gheorghe Adrian, a Moldavian, became Minister of War for Wallachia. However, given a tense diplomatic situation owing to the reluctance of Turkey and Austria to recognize the double election of Prince Cuza, it was essential to unite both armies under a single command.[5] This was accomplished by Order of the Day No. 98 issued in Bucharest in 1860 which established a single War Ministry and one Commander in Chief in the person of Colonel Ion Emanoil Florescu. Thus the army became the first major governmental institution to be unified two years before a unitary state was established (1862). Thus the initial reform and organization of the Romanian army took place during the period when Florescu was at the helm. We quote from the study written by General Radu Rosetti, a foremost military historian, who attempts to summarize all that was accomplished:[6]

> *"There is no chapter in our military formation which does not bear the marks of Florescu: the union of the armies, the creation of the General Staff, the union of the military schools in Iasi and Bucharest, sharing the new flags that bear the arms of the united country, the organization of the Upper Staff of the Ministry of War, the foundation of the permanent Council in charge of training the army, the intendancies and the administrative officers corps, setting up of new army corps, the artillery regiment, field troops, the corps of engineers, the establishment of the sanitary service, the creation of a ammunition factory, the armory and powder mills, its personnel; the cavalry, the army children: fencing, gymnastics and target practice schools; the unification of the navy and the military courts, the reorganization of the administration, the firemen, dorobanti and graniceri departments; all those reforms were accomplished if not under the initiative of Florescu while he was a Minister of War, at least with his complete collaboration."*
>
> Actually, Florescu took part in most of the army reforms even when he was not Minister of War.[7]

He was also involved in issues concerning the Romanian army as Minister of Internal Affairs, Public Works and Agriculture, and a Senator in the Romanian Parliament although all the General's decisions bore Prince Cuza's signature, the official head of state. Even though Prince Cuza had

[5]Ibidem, year I, (1860), no. 21 (June 3), pages 321-322.
[6]Ibidem, year I (1860), no. 27 (July 30), page 419.
[7]General Rosetti, Un uitat…, page 11.

been a soldier in the Moldavian army at a young age, he ended his military career as Minister of War of Moldavia. However, Cuza's military experience was shallow. The American historian Thad Weed Riker, author of a brilliant monograph on the Cuza period, wrote that Florescu was the most valuable man among Cuza's intimates.[8] King Carol I, who hardly ever spoke highly of his advisers, readily acknowledged Florescu's contributions by appointing him Minister of War, (1871-75). Baligot de Beyne, the Prince's secretary, in a letter addressed to Iancu Alecsandri, Cuza's diplomatic agent in Paris wrote: "*Florescu in the only genuine military man; he loves his work.*" (September 3, 1862).[9]

When discussing Florescu's modernization of the army we should not forget he was the product of French military training.[10] As a former student of the French General Staff School, Florescu maintained his contacts with Paris as well as with the representatives of the government of Napoleon III in Iasi and Bucharest.

France after all represented a great military power at the time and it was in the interest of both countries to work together. The French military mission in the Romanian Principalities was led by lieutenant colonel Eugène Lamy with his brother Emile Lamy, and the superintendent Guy le Cler, accompanied by an entire officers' team. They were helped by a number of Romanian officers who also completed their education at French military centers. The relationships between the French officers and Florescu's team were correct, but sometimes there were certain tensions between the two, as the French considered themselves superior to Romanian officers.[11]

In his reports to the Ministry of Defense, Eugène Lamy often complained about the lack of understanding shown by Romanian officers. Nonetheless he had a good opinion of General Florescu whom he considered a reliable ally as a student at the General Staff School in Paris: "*A former student of our General Staff School, gifted with a brilliant intelligence, very active and animated by the passionate wish to be useful to his country, he spent his time and efforts to accelerate the implementation of our training and administrative system. He is one of the few Wallachian*

[8]T. W. Riker, The Making of Romania. A Study of an International problem 1855-1856, Oxford, 1931, page 12. Also see R.V. Bossy, Agentia diplomatica a Romanian la Paris, p. 122.

[9]"Florescu est le seul vrai militaire; il est trop gentleman, trop bon enfant avec ses officers. C'est son seul tort. Il a l'amour du métier, l'activite, l'amour propre, l'initiative," see Academic Romana, MSS, I. Alecsandri, 2nd series, vol. II, p. 249. Also see Maria Georgescu, Misiunea militara franceza in Romania, in Anuarul Institutului pentru Studii Politice de Istorie Militara," Bucharest, 1977, p. 714.

[10]Maria Gerogescu, ibidem, Bucharest, page 198.

[11]E. Lamy was in charge with the vanatori and target shooting regiments under Prince Carol's rule, see Maria Georgescu, ibidem, page 203.

boyars who welcomes us with sympathy and the only one I could find ready to help the French Mission."

Though Eugène Lamy spoke highly of the Romanian non-commissioned officers educated in France, he criticized their superiors from the General Staff who were often unprepared, indolent and conceited. It was obvious that the French officers encouraged reforms aimed at turning Romania into an ally of France. Nonetheless one should not forget that they were "technical advisers" of the army, only allowed to make "recommendations." Their advice was taken seriously and they made substantial contributions in the reorganization of the Romanian army. In any event, each decision required General Florescu's approval. To do this Florescu kept up contacts with his colleagues in Paris, most of all with Marshal Count Randon, the Minister of War. Though often seeking his advice, he did not always follow it, despite all the sympathy that he had for France.

The head of the French Military Mission, Eugène Lamy eventually returned to France at the end of Cuza's rule, half satisfied with the results achieved but somewhat blamed General Florescu for not being strict enough to win the sympathy of his high-ranking officers. His brother, Emile Lamy, continued his activity even after Prince Carol had hired a team of German officers.

In order to completely understand the main directions of General Florescu's reforms in his first period at the helm of the Ministry of War we should quote from "*Monitorul Oastei*" (The Army Journal) founded by Florescu and from his own words printed in Bucharest, i.e., "*Presentation of the most important improvements within the army of the United Principalities ever since January 24, 1859 until June 1, 1861*" in which the general essentially summarized the reforms accomplished during the first year of his tenure.[12] His main task was to unify the Moldavian and the Wallachian armies which had distinctive features of their own.

Many of the boyar families in the Principalities still hoped that Cuza's election would remain an isolated event and they would eventually return to the former situation. On the other hand many unionists placed their hopes on the election of a foreign prince. At first mutual visits made by the Moldavian regiments in Bucharest and by the Wallachian regiments in Iasi followed by frequent exchanges had a symbolic significance. The united command, which was eventually set up in Bucharest, the organization of a combined General Staff made up of high-ranking officers from both Principalities, the organization of joint administrative services, and heads of the army corps, all progressively became homogenous in 1859-1866.

A good example of this fusion was the Criminal Code of the Moldavian army. In February 1860 Prince Cuza had signed an order according to which "*the armies in both Principalities should adopt the*

---

[12]Stephan Rassidescu National Printing House, Bucharest 1861.

Criminal Code of Wallachia while the Garrison Service Code continues to be that of Moldavia until the new regulations were drafted."[13] The united command, which was eventually set up in Bucharest, the organization of a combined General Staff made up of high-ranking officers from both Principalities, the organization of united administrative services as well as heads of the army corps; all of these were accomplished during the 1859-61 period with Moldavia and Wallachia officers serving side by side in Bucharest. Florescu also established a Central Revision Command.

Another task at least as important as the progressive establishment of a single army administration was that of making army service attractive to the peasants so as to increase the number of recruits. In the past peasants considered army service as a kind of servitude; they were badly paid, poorly quartered and lived in humiliating conditions. Recruiting itself was difficult and many of the enlisted men abandoned their posts. An important measure was the abolition of the title of "Junker" imposed by the Russians for boyar officers. General Florescu therefore initiated a number of regulations concerning the promotion of soldiers and non-commissioned officers. From this point onward promotion in rank was accessible to any soldier depending on his abilities. In March 1862 General Florescu presented a bill comprising 24 articles to the Romanian Parliament establishing a military hierarchy modeled upon that of France: General, Colonel, Lieutenant Colonel, Major, Captain, Lieutenant, Second Lieutenant, Sergeant-Major, Sergeant, Corporal and Private. The law explained the criteria for promotion from one rank to another, but in Napoleonic terms an army career was open to talent and promotion was possible for any talented private.[14]

General Florescu was very concerned in maintaining adequate living conditions for the wives, orphans, and children of impoverished soldiers. For this purpose he created (Decree 46, March 6th, 1861) a unit of troop children and wives, four children and two wives in each infantry company, cavalry squadron and artillery unit. Children from age 12 onward were placed under the care of a sergeant while the wives worked in kitchens and laundries. In order to improve morale the General had rewards for soldiers who distinguished themselves and enlisted for additional years in the army and he set up an endowment to reward them. Another fund was established for the disabled.

The reorganization of the Romanian army during General Florescu's initial tenure in office took place one step at a time, mostly during the initial 1860-1861 period. Army administration was tackled in a report to Prince

---

[13]M.O. (Wallachia) year I, 1860, no. 4 (February 27), page 449.

[14]The bill concerning the military hierarchy presented by General Florescu devised the rank of lieutenant colonel for the military instructors of the French Mission who were attached to the Romanian army. It also provided for the two classes of generals: division general and brigade general.

Cuza on May 1860. The general decreed the creation of a Board of Directors for the various army units. Article 14 specified that the Board of Directors of an army corps would be composed of a colonel-president, a captain and accounting officers.[15] That of a battalion would consist of the battalion commander, a captain and an accountant appointed by the Board. If the unit was smaller than a battalion the head of the corps would assume the responsibilities of the Board of Directors. In each instance the leadership of the unit would be replaced every year by the officer who followed in terms of length of service or seniority. Disciplinary units were established by an Order of the Day, in May 1860.

Other regulations followed with an eye to the minutest details. For instance, the specific duties of a regimental commander; the manner in which an army clerk should answer a questionnaire, writing rules for army chancelleries, examinations of army engineers, regulations for target shooting (a hobby of his), physical exercise, were all closely watched by a man who considered himself above all an army educator. There were even rules concerning the lighting of barracks and sentry posts, transportation costs of army goods, setting up accountant and cashier centers. Army pay was carefully scrutinized with lower salaries for soldiers on vacation or those hospitalized. Every item concerning a soldier's life was kept under Florescu's close scrutiny.

Military music particularly was an object of particular concern. In a letter addressed to Vasile Alecsandri (November 8, 1860), Florescu wrote: *"History shows that all over the world music and poetry represent means of uplifting the soldiers' spirits for prince and country. Nowadays all the nations have a national anthem which they sing during battles for the glory of their country. In this respect, it has been two months now since I promised a 100 piaster prize for the person who will compose a national anthem...." I have not yet thought of the words because I have always admired your poetic genius and patriotism. Undoubtedly your muse is the Romanians' favorite muse and your songs are our soldiers' favorite songs. I am certain that you will not refuse my request to offer the army such an anthem because you are ready to do anything for our great army. I shall not make any suggestions concerning length, rhythm or lyrics. It would be better if they followed the pattern below which is far from being appropriate to our purpose. I am looking forward for an answer to my request which I have made on behalf of the United Principalities Army."*[16]

---

[15]The debates of the Senate and of the Romanian General Assembly (1864-1865), pages 350-351: according to Article 10 of the laws concerning pensions, widows of soldiers who died in service received half of the pension as long as they did not get married again. Also see Elena Palanceanu work, Cu privire la masurile lui Alexandru Iozn Cuza, 1859-1861, p. 133.

[16]M.O., Ibidem, year I (1860), no. 36 (September 30), page 565; no. 4 (February 27), pages 52-53; "Monitorul Oficial al Romaniei," no. 77 (supplement), session XXXV, of February 19, 1863, page 4.

Dumitru Florescu, the General's nephew, eventually composed this anthem called "Hora Unirii," based on Alecsandri's lyrics.

In the first quarter of 1862 Parliament initiated a series of debates intended to augment the number of troops and establish an army budget. The Committee was initially composed of Nicolae Bibescu, Mihail Kogalniceanu, Nicolae Mavrocordat, Grigore Argiropulo with General Florescu the secretary of the drafting committee. Its work encompassed all aspects of army reform. It resulted in a number of laws passed in 1862, 1864 and 1865, numerous decrees and Orders of the Day bearing Florescu's signature. Although General Florescu's incumbency at the War Office ended in 1864 in his capacity of Commander in Chief of the Army under Cuza and as Minister of the Interior in 1865 (but mostly as one of the parliamentarians most familiar with military affairs), his influence in army reform was paramount.

Florescu had always considered the infantry the most important unit of the army on future battlefields. It was, therefore, essential to increase the number of regiments in that branch. Initially two regiments of the line were added, one in Moldavia, the other in Wallachia. In addition a fourth and fifth line regiments were added in Wallachia and another in Moldavia. A 7th regiment was created by the Council of Ministers in October 1860.[17]

By an Order of the Day in October 1860 which concerned the entire dorobanti corps, General Florescu regulated many details regarding the administration of that body of troops whom he clearly desired to keep under the authority of the War Ministry. In 1864 when disturbances against the Cuza regime started to erupt in various parts of the country, General Florescu introduced the idea of a civic guard, that of an inactive militia and peasant infantry units. The same law provided military training for young men who graduated from the compulsory elementary schools. Instruction for peasant infantry units was also provided by Florescu when he took charge of the Ministry of Internal Affairs in 1865.

The Military Law of 1865 reaffirmed the disposition subordinating the dorobanti, gendarmes, graniceri (henceforth called militias) to the War Office thus becoming part of the territorials. The General also decided to divide the army of the Principalities into four divisions one stationed in Bucharest, the others in Iasi, Galati and Craiova. Military service became compulsory for all citizens, four years in regular service and two years in the reserves. Maneuvers for the new recruits took place every year during autumn.

In turn the cavalry increased its establishment in 1860 with two additional squadrons which formed together with the lancer unit in Moldavia the 2nd cavalry regiment. At the time General Florescu handed to the Prince a report asking him to endow these regiments with remount

---

[17]M.O., (Wallachia) Ibidem, year I (1860), no. 20 (May 30), page 350; no. 51 (December 18), page 890; year II (1861), no. 1 (January 4), pages 3-13.

officers and stables for the horses ordered from abroad. He also decided to establish a cavalry school with a distinguished director and specialist in equestrian style. A mountain corps battalion was also founded during that initial period when the 3rd battalion of the fifth infantry regiment of Moldavia became a distinctive unit of its own with an appropriate military staff trained in mountain warfare.[18]

With his Crimean war experience Florescu paid a good deal of attention to the necessity of establishing a sanitary unit together with a hospital for sick or disabled soldiers. He also foresaw the need of a hierarchy of rank for the medical corps under the leadership of a director of high competence. On his proposal Dr. Charles Davila, a French citizen who had resided in the Principalities for some time and was married to a Romanian, was appointed Director of the Joint Sanitary Services of the Romanian army with the rank of General. It was further stipulated (Order of the Day, No. 96, May 26, 1860) that every infantry company should appoint an officer who must attend special courses offered by the sanitary service.[19] The two existing Danubian gunboats belonging to Moldavia and Wallachia were also united into a single fleet in October 1860. Henceforth they were to operate as a joint naval force under one commander. Their duty was to study defensive possibilities in the Principalities both on the Danube and on the Sulina channel under the supervision of the Danubian Commission following the Crimean war. General Florescu was interested in equipping this small naval force with new warships, a well trained staff and well equipped bases. On that score he fought repeatedly with the Parliamentarians but had to wait until 1869 when he was no longer in power to see the first warship built. He was convinced that endowing the country with an appropriate flotilla would prove essential in securing the country's frontiers *vis a vis* Bulgaria, at the time still an integral part of the Ottoman Empire. In addition, a fleet would help secure international commerce on the Danube which increased immeasurably following the fall of the Russian Protectorate.

Tall, good looking, sporting a Napoleonic moustache and beard, General Florescu had a passion for uniforms and paid a good deal of attention to the sartorial elegance of his new army. Having served in a French regiment he had a predilection for the colorful uniforms of his second fatherland, though he was also inspired by the more gaudy costumes of other lands. In a speech delivered in 1861 the general stated that for him the uniform was a matter of "national pride."[20]

The first step was to remove the differences which existed between the uniforms of Moldavia and Wallachia. Thus a mixed Moldo-Wallachian

---

[18]M.O. (the official newspaper of the United Principalities), year I (1860), no. 37 (October 8), page 583; General Florescu, Espunere de imbunatatire…, page 13.

[19]"Monitorul Oastei" (Wallachia), year I (1860), no. 4 (February 27), page 50.

[20]Cristian M. Vladescu, Uniformele armatei romane, Bucharest, 1977, page 56.

committee was appointed as early as March 20, 1859 and debates lasted until 1864 when we can speak of the elaboration of a single uniform for both Moldavian and Wallachian armies. Florescu decreed that henceforth soldiers and officers of all arms: infantry, cavalry, artillery, the fireman corps, mountain troops, granicer, dorobanti, army physicians, musicians, the navy, officers of the general staff, Ministry of War personnel, be compelled to wear a uniform. These were designed by a commission in which the General had the principal role. As part of the new standardization all uniform buttons bore the emblems of both Principalities: the auroch's head for Moldavia and the eagle for Wallachia. Interestingly enough the first soldiers to actually wear these newly designed uniforms were the army physicians, also called "sanitary officers of the United Principalities." Although the hierarchy of rank was similar to those of other officers, they were not allowed to wear epaulettes as a sign of seniority.

With regards to the officer corps, Florescu set up regulations distinguishing rank on the sleeves of tunics, caps and greatcoats--the basic color being dark blue with golden embroideries. A double red stripe covered the dark blue trousers worn on formal occasions while the light grey trousers for daily wear only had a single stripe. The epaulettes for all ranks were woven with golden threads and had an embroidered plaque with geometrical motifs and garland spirals on the ring-shaped piece; thick fringes hanged from these embroideries. The highest ranks were distinguished by five cornered white stars: two for division general, one for Brigadier general. All generals wore epaulettes with an engraved metal plaque bearing the image of a sun with a white star on the side. A red cloth cape was adopted for the entire army with a branch of oak leaves on the collar: two branches for division generals and one for general-captains.

As the work of the committee on army standardization progressed Florescu took personal responsibility in sketching the new uniforms for all branches of the new army and often changed his mind. For instance, while he initially adopted dark blue tunics and light grey trousers for the line infantry regiments, he changed his mind in 1861 and favored a red cloth uniform. A uniform was also introduced for the military school for both officers and administrative directors.

First and foremost a cavalry officer Florescu adopted a single uniform for this corps made up of lancers and dorobanti as early as 1859 though he later submitted a variety of new designs for his favorite arm: the lancers were to adopt a short blue tunic and riding trousers worn under a grey cloth cape with rolled-up collar and tabs, with a distinctive whitish hue. The riding dorobanti were also given a new tunic: black cloth with hems and cords of golden threads on the shoulders, white cloth trousers, boots with fixed spurs, an astrakhan hat with egret and a yellow cap resembling that of the lancers. In 1864, this uniform was modified by new regulations.

In 1860 Florescu established the uniform for the artillery. The cloth was blue, with edges striped red, and the distinctive mark on the arm was a grenade showing a bomb with flames in seven colors marked on the corners of the collar. The following year in January 1861, he regulated the mountain corps' uniform: black hat, brown tunic, black trousers, boots and white leggings. The trumpeters wore a woolen lace around the collars and cuffs, worked in tricolor (red, yellow, blue). The blacksmiths wore on the sleeve of their tunic and vest, a horseshoe made of red cloth between shoulder and elbow.

For the engineering battalions founded in 1861 (Report No. 4686/1861) Florescu described the uniforms as follows: blue cloth tunic, trousers of the same color, with two red stripes with slight modifications for the various types of dress. The fireman's uniform was also regulated: dark blue tunic and trousers with red stripes, but one braid only. Their distinguishing mark was a brass plaque on the front side of the helmet, with two crossed axes and a ribbon with the words, "Firemen Corps." A series of orders of the day were signed by General Florescu in the second half of 1860 and the first half of the following year. They provided uniforms for army bread contractors, the intendency personnel and brass musical bands. Special uniforms were to be worm by all members of the armed forces on Sunday and national holidays with distinctive epaulettes, sashes, hats, according to arm; there were also mourning outfits for officers, non-commissioned officers, corporals and privates.

In 1864 General Florescu finalized the design of the uniforms for formal ceremonial wear as well as office and daily wear (mufti) though his work could not be considered complete until 1871-73, when he was once again at the helm of the War Office. The latest models ordered abroad were finally completed. In conclusion, it might be said that during this whole period Florescu succeeded in designing the uniforms of the "new army" often depicted on the canvasses of famous painters who witnessed the War of Independence.

More important than an elegant army was the task of securing weaponry. In a letter addressed to Cuza by Napoleon III in 1861 the Prince stated, "On my accession to the throne of the United Principalities the army possessed only four or five thousand Russian rifles dating back to the days of Empress Catherine of Russia's rule and about ten worthless Russian and Austrian canons. We could not fire one shot without their permission…."[21]

Prince Cuza was evidently intent upon improving the country's defenses and endowing the troops with appropriate weapons in sufficient quantities. For this purpose when he sent Vasile Alecsandri and Stefan Golescu in 1859 on a mission to obtain the recognition of the union of the Principalities by the European governments, he also instructed them to

[21]Gheorghe I. Bratianu, Politica externa a lui Cuza Voda si dezvoltarea ideii de unitate nationala, Bucharest, 1932, pages 136-137.

purchase updated weapons under favorable conditions. Napoleon III was sympathetic to their plea and decided to donate chassepot rifles with the necessary ammunitions as a gift to the Romanian army. The material was to be shipped by boat to the port of Galati. That year 25,000 rifles were indeed unloaded in Piedmontese boats on the pier of that port. General Florescu was able to report to the Prince that in addition to the rifles, sufficient cannons for two artillery batteries had also arrived, as well as swords for the cavalry.

In addition to obtaining weaponry abroad Florescu decided it was equally important to manufacture the arms within the country. With this end in view a decision was made to build an arsenal at Malmaison--the land having been purchased by auction. This new edifice and its outbuildings represented the first step in the creation of a native armament industry which enhanced the military preparedness within the country.[22] Another munitions factory was built with Belgian help in addition to the powder works at Cotroceni. For expertise, Romanian artillery officers were sent to study at the pyrotechnics school in Antwerp. By the end of 1860 Captain, soon-to-be-Major, Henrick Herckt an artillery officer of Flemish origin serving in the Romanian army was also sent to study methods of producing percussion caps.

With the help of another Belgian Lieutenant Le Boulange, Florescu drew a project for a third smaller munitions factory. This was approved by Parliament in 1861 when the necessary machinery and equipment was ordered at the Lachausse and Jormiaux plants in Liege and shipped from Antwerp to Galati in 1861.[23] Pyrotechnic works were built in Bucharest at Curtea Arsa and Spirei Hill in the spring of 1862. All these munitions factories were eventually placed under the order of Major Herckt.

With the support of patriotic politicians General Florescu succeeded in acquiring additional foreign imported weaponry: 13,093 chassepot rifles from France with percussion caps for the infantry, 30,000 for the cavalry, 6,298 for the Alpine troops, 700 pistols in all, 4,314 swords for the cavalry, 1,998 sabers for the infantry, 1,600 spears, 46 bronze artillery pieces, caliber 4 and 12, together with canon balls. In addition to French munitions General Florescu was perceptive enough to recognize the superiority of German Krupp artillery pieces (75 and 105 mm) which were purchased on the advice of Romanian artillery officers, Coanda, Rudeanu and Ghenea. The later invented panoramic field glasses subsequently adopted by all the armies of the world. Thus, with Prince Cuza's help Florescu had succeeded in creating the beginnings of a national army equipped with adequate weaponry of its own.

Fully conscious of the extent of reliance on French army supplies Prince Cuza addressed a letter to Napoleon III in 1864. He explained that

---

[22]Documente privind Unirea principatelor..., page 543.
[23]General Florescu, Espunere de imbunatatire, page 21.

when he was elected Prince of the United Principalities, *"I found 13,000 people recruited exclusively from peasants, badly armed, badly equipped and who obeyed Russian and Austrian orders. Today I have 12,000 graniceri, 8,000 foot and riding gendarmes and a regular army of 20,000 men recruited from all social classes. I have a very well equipped army and am able to increase its establishments three times by calling to arms a reserve which is twice as big and which was trained at the great school of military principles."*[24] These numbers were increased mostly by the 1864 law which concerned the army organization. The new army of 20,000 men included the permanent army with its reserves and the militias made up of graniceri and dorobanti together with their reserves. Those comprised seven line infantry regiments, three battalions of vanatori, one disciplinary company, three cavalry regiments, and one artillery regiment with six batteries, two companies with train of units, one engineering battalion and one medical unit. Although the new army could not be considered as being able to wage an offensive war, its power could at least secure the frontiers of the United Principalities. That was hardly the case during the period of the Regime of the Organic Statute when military actions were limited to only police activity.

In his attempts to increase the number of soldiers and to acquire the necessary weapons, General Florescu confronted the hostility and lack of understanding of certain members of Parliament who opposed him on both on political and personal grounds. He was certainly not a great orator nor able to use the flowery language popular at the time to impress an audience of the period. His message was invariably brief but rarely passionate. He sometimes wasted a good deal of time on points concerning army detail. A good instance occurred during a debate which took place during the session of February 1861 when Florescu suggested that the head of the Danubian flotilla be placed under the command of an officer with the rank of colonel. He pleaded with his colleagues in the following manner: "Gentlemen appoint if not a colonel at least a lieutenant-colonel; our flotilla is called upon to increase in size....moreover, the fleet will also be able to be used for the transportation of grain and in addition ensure the security of our country, certainly a worthy cause."[25]

This particular debate ended with the rejection of Florescu's request even though in the end a compromise was reached. Paying a Colonel's salary was judged excessive for the fleet commander. The rank of major was considered sufficient for the fleet command, in terms of the military budget a petty economy. However Florescu succeeded in this particular debate in securing the salary he suggested for the director of the military press – 800 leis a month and 400 for his two assistants. On the other hand,

---

[24]M. O. (Wallachia) an I (1860), no. 4 (February 27), page 64.

[25]"Monitorul Oficial al Romaniei," supplement to no. 71, pages 1-3; supplement to no. 72, session XXXVIII, February 22, 1863, page 6.

the General was compelled to give up his request for a director of the musical bandmaster and was forced to reduce the number of troop children and wives allocated for army duty.

Besides being the army's organizer, General Florescu also became involved in training his troops during his years in office. He spent a great deal of time inspecting garrisons on the parade ground. He also reviewed soldiers during field maneuvers which generally took place in autumn so that the recruits would gain the experience in simulating actual battle conditions. The general's "Orders of the Day" can be followed in detail by reading the *Army Monitor*. Many foreign observers such as the Duke of Brabant the heir to the Belgian throne on a visit to Bucharest in March 1860 were favorably impressed by such exercises.[26] This impression was later confirmed when the Duke traveled to Jassy where he watched an actual full exercise by the artillery under the direction of General Milicescu who directed the fire at certain preselected targets with speed and accuracy. During an inspection made of the Lancers and other cavalry regiments General Florescu also had words of praise. One ambitious maneuver on a larger scale took place on July 21 and August 1 both at the Floreasca camp near Bucharest on the border of the Colentina Lake under the command of General Macedonski. The tactical theme of the maneuvers was issued by General Florescu. The latter accepted the advice of Colonel Eugene Lamy who criticized Florescu being somewhat piqued by the fact that he had not been given the important role he expected. In September 1863 when tricolor flags were being distributed to the troops Prince Guza spoke to the assembled officers and men. "This flag stands for Romania; it represents our past, our present and the future of our country; our whole history. In a word the flag stands for all our military responsibilities and virtues by words carved on the eagles of the Roman legions: Honor and Fatherland."[27]

In 1859 following Cuza's double election, a delicate diplomatic problem threatened to jeopardize the very existence of the Union since neither the Habsburg nor Turkish Empire had sanctioned Cuza's double election. *De jure*, the Turkish Sultan still represented the suzerain power. Both governments requested the summoning of an international conference protesting what they determined a violation of the terms of the Paris Convention of 1858 which had specifically required the maintenance of two separate Princes.

The work of the Conference at Constantinople began on March 26/April 7, 1859. Costache Negri Cuza's representative kept him posted on developments at a time when the Turks were beginning to concentrate their troops at Sumla for an eventual intervention on Romanian soil. The situation in Bucharest was tense as the government realized the possibility

[26]Ibidem, supplement to no. 72 (February 16) 1863, pages 102.
[27]M.O. (Wallachia), year I (1860), no. 9 (March 26), page 129; no. 13 (April 9), page 197; no. 14 (April 21), page 221; no. 15 (May 3) page 225.

of an armed Turkish invasion. This danger may well have hastened Cuza's decision to unite the two armies before the formal union of the Principalities was officially declared. Even though the two armies were not as yet joined into a single force, but to assuage sensibilities, Cuza decided to place the Moldavian force under a Wallachian officer, namely General Florescu, while the Moldavian army, as previously noted, was placed under General Adrian.

The next step was that of concentrating both Moldavian and Wallachian forces at Floresti, a good strategic location between Ploesti and Campina. Both forces were placed under the command of General Florescu. This position enabled Florescu to march towards the Danube where the Turkish army was positioned towards Transylvania where an Austrian intervention was possible. Initially the operation involved a Moldavian infantry regiment as well as the 12th Wallachian infantry unit under the command of General Florescu and General Milicescu. The two forces fraternized in an atmosphere which was festive and enthusiastic. Eventually a significant number of men were added at the Floresti camp involving additional units of both armies, ten line battalions with 750 soldiers each, 6 lancer squadrons with 170 cavalry men and 7 dorobanti companies with 180 solders. Doctor Davila was entrusted with the sanitary unit.

Fortunately for Romania the threatened conflict never came to a head. Austria's defeat by the Franco-Piedmontese armies impelled Austria and Turkey to accept the decision of Great Britain, Russian, France and the Kingdom of Savoy to accept the double election of Prince Cuza. Because of the good relations which existed with the new Kingdom of Sardinia General Florescu sent a military mission henceforth attached to the Piedmontese army.

Once union was proclaimed, General Florescu was determined to use the new army to protect the frontiers of the United Principalities against whatever force threatened the integrity of the new state. This also applied to infractions committed by Ottoman irregular troops for the most part that crossed the Danube without any order from the Ottoman government. A lieutenant Mihaescu was in charge of frontier outposts and opened fire on the Turks. On that occasion Florescu issued an "Order of the Day" addressed to the whole Romanian army (February 4, 1860) in which he expressed the view that whenever trespassers violated Romanian territory, "border guards shall respond with fire."[28] If they were unable to resist they must appeal to neighboring units to help the offensive.

Frontier units reacted in a similar manner in another incident involving the landing of Austrian sailors on Danubian gunboats who violated Moldavian soil and exchanged fire with a frontier police unit.[29] The

---

[28]M.O., year I (1860), no. 45 (November 19), pages 764-776; no. 51 (December 19) pages 909-910, supplement to no. 51, pages 922-924.

[29]The Romanian Academy, Cuza Archives, XXLIX, pages 322-323.

incident was without importance but General Florescu telegraphed the commander of the Craiova unit to investigate the incident and make a report. He ended his report with the following words: "How come our soldiers did not find out sooner about this incident and did not alert the troops to arrest all the sailors?"[30]

Far more significant was an incident involving the forcible entry of a Polish revolutionary force on Romanian territory in July 1863 possibly on their way to Poland one year before the outbreak of the Polish revolution against Russia in 1864.[31] Understandably Prince Cuza like so many former forty-eighters sympathized with Poland's struggle for freedom from Russia. Many Poles had, like the Romanians, fought on the revolutionary barricades of Paris and were friends of Lamartine the French poet who also befriended the Romanians in Paris. At first glance the Romanian reaction was to keep a blind eye with the hope that the Poles would soon be out of the country without hostile intent. It was only the moment when the Polish commander Milkowski made use of firearms as he crossed the Romanian border that the Romanian guards were forced to return fire. When the incident was reported to Bucharest, General Florescu ordered the local commander Colonel Calinescu to "take the most serious measures in order to stop the Polish violation of Romanian territory. When you encounter these forces challenge them to surrender their weapons and turn back. Should you encounter resistance, hold your own and use gun fire."[32]

The Polish commander refused the General's request and a battle ensued at Costanglia during some five hours with casualties on both sides. Though the Poles were superior in number, the smaller Romanian force compelled them to withdraw. Colonel Calinescu pursued the Poles and forced them to surrender in the village of Ranzesti. The Polish Romanian incident was the most important armed conflict in which the new Romanian army was involved and proved an embarrassment in Polish-Romanian relations. The Poles were eventually allowed to regain their homeland though Colonel Milkowski later acknowledged the folly of his action. Both Prince Cuza and Florescu's reaction could be explained in part by the fact that they were both aware of Napoleon III opposition to the Polish revolution of 1863 against Russia.

Another problem which faced Cuza's government was the security of Romania's fishermen in the Danube delta – the Danube lying under the protection of the International Commission of the Allied Powers following the Crimean War. In 1865 General Florescu sent Major Sachelarie, a representative of the Finance Ministry, to collaborate with the members of

[30]The Romanian Academy, Cuza Archives III, p. 620; Constantin C. Giurescu, Alexandru Ioan Cuza, pages 31-32.

[31]Documents concerning the Union of the Principalities, III, Bucharest, 1996, pages 652-653.

[32]"Monitorul Oastei at Romaniei," year I 1860, no. 20 (May 30) page 305.

the International Danubian Commission protecting the rights and livelihood of the Romanian fishermen so often ignored.[33]

Other incidents concerning Romania's external relations such as the attempts of Mazzini's International Revolutionary Committee in London to induce the Romanians to join forces in rekindling the revolutionary movement of 1848 aroused little interest even though Prince Cuza, a former revolutionary, could not but sympathize with their objectives. General Florescu on the other hand, a moderate conservative, would under no circumstances involve the Romanian army in supporting a movement he had always disavowed.

A much more serious matter concerned the attempt of Prince Milan Obrenovic to smuggle Russian weapons (63,000 rifles equipped with bayonets, 30 artillery pieces, and 3,000 swords) to Serbia, an action which became known to the Protecting Powers and occasioned a formal protest by their consular representatives. This action evidently represented a violation of the United Principalities' sovereignty-- a neutral state. The problem was all the more delicate since Cuza's mistress Maria Obrenovic was the daughter of Costin Catargiu, a Romanian citizen. In any event, Cuza, just as General Florescu, had great sympathy for the young Serbian State which shared identical ideals with those of the United Principalities, namely, that of eventually winning total independence from Ottoman rule.

The problem was finally resolved by Cuza and Florescu making use of diplomatic niceties. Soothing reassurances were delivered to the Austro-Hungarian consul in Bucharest to the effect that no arms would be allowed to cross Romanian territory. Nevertheless, somehow the weapons reached their destination in secret. Proof of the matter was the gift of a sword offered by Prince Milosevic to Prince Cuza with the inscription "amico certo in re incerta."[34] Another sword and medal were offered by the Serbian Prince to Florescu, both of which are still in the family's possession.

Besides being the closest collaborator of Prince Cuza, General Florescu was also one of his faithful politically allies. As a moderate conservative the General believed that the duty of a Minister of War during the absence of the Prince required an effective police force to maintain order within the country: "It is absolutely necessary," wrote Florescu to Cuza, "for the State to take strong action with the help of its armed forces so as not to be reduced to powerlessness in moments of anarchy."

At the beginning of Cuza's rule, the United Principalities were threatened by various problems: insubordination during recruiting operations, peasants asking for land reform, separatist forces in each Principality, refusal to pay taxes, discontent among the guilds, refusal among many to accept Cuza's rule. The danger of a revolution against the

[33]The Romanian Academy, Cuza Archives IX, p. 116; XVIII, p. 125-126; XXII, p. 14.
[34]The Romanian Academy, Cuza Archives, XXVIII, p. 5; Constantin C. Giurescu, Viata si opera..., page 178; Independenta Romaniei, pages 111-112.

regime was always present. In a letter addressed to Cuza in 1862 Florescu informed the Prince that he disposed of an infantry battalion, a squadron of lancers, firemen, police and gendarmes that could be mobilized at a moment's notice in the vicinity of Bucharest if necessary. The so-called "monstrous coalition" radical and conservatives against Cuza was also in the making by 1862 and Florescu advised Cuza to consider the possibility of resorting to Napoleon style "coup d'etat" to strengthen the authority of the Prince and to thwart the impending conspiracy. Hints of the kind were given by Florescu to the Prince: "The Assembly has just taken a ten day vacation. I wish it were to last as long as possible for the welfare of our State," a hint which Cuza took to heart later.[35]

At the time of Prince Cuza's accession the two most pressing problems concerned the emancipation of the serfs and the distribution of land to the peasants and the secularization of the Greek monasteries dedicated to Mount Athos and a number of other Orthodox Bishoprics the incomes of which were sent abroad – a substantial loss of revenue for the country. Since the conservative government of Lascar Catargiu was vehemently opposed to any concession to the peasant class, this raised the specter of revolutionary action as in the days of Tudor Vladimirescu's uprising of 1821 as peasants began marching towards Bucharest.

Facing this danger Florescu was always ready to use the army to quell any disturbance as he had done in 1860 when Cuza faced the opposition of the liberals in Parliament. Clashes took place; some of the peasant leaders were arrested and imprisoned at Vacaresti and there were casualties. With the assassination of Barbu Catargiu in June 1862 the head of the conservative government Cuza at first attempted to appoint Nicolae Cretulescu, a moderate conservative, friendly to General Florescu and opposed to the radical groups who were already preparing "the monstrous coalition" against Cuza's regime. In the end (October 1863) Cuza appointed Mihail Kogalniceanu premier with the task of secularizing the Greek monastic estates and promulgating agrarian reform which set the peasants free from feudal charges and allotted them some of the Boyars land.

These reforms could only have been achieved when the Prince finally took Florescu's hint and engineered his famous *coup d'etat* followed by a plebiscite which dissolved the unruly Assembly and strengthened his personal rule (May 1864). Kogalniceanu's appointment signified Florescu's dismissal from the War Ministry largely because of his use of the army in quelling peasant disorders. Although General Alexander Iachovache was now at the helm of the War Office, General Florescu continued to be Commander in Chief of the army and Prince Cuza declared himself entirely satisfied with Florescu's actions.

With the fall of the Kogalniceanu government in 1865, the moderate conservative Nicolae Cretulescu once again became Prime Minister (July

---

[35]See appendix.

14). General Florescu was then appointed Minister of the Interior, Public Works and Agriculture, and interim President of the Council of Ministers, a most important post, while his friend General Manu was Minister of War.[36] Prince Cuza, whose health was failing, thought the situation was secure enough to take a cure abroad at the watering resort of Ems in Germany. The liberal opposition and their conservative allied members of the "monstrous coalition" then decided to take advantage of the Prince's absence to attempt a *coup d'etat* of their own by inciting the citizenry of Bucharest, merchants, artisans, storekeepers to revolt against certain unpopular measures that Cuza had taken such as state monopoly of the tobacco industry. Posters were placed in the capital and pamphlets circulated accusing the privileged "thieves," mostly members of the Cuza camarilla which included the Prince's Director of the Posts and Telegraphy Librecht and his mistress Maria Obrenovici of fleecing the people. The revolutionaries made certain to draw the attention of the foreign press to such altercations. The plotters desired to remove Cuza from the throne for an additional reason. They believed that a prestigious foreign prince would be more apt to obtain total independence from the Turks. Emissaries, notably Ion Bratianu, had been sent to Germany to negotiate with the prestigious Hohenzollern Sigmaringen family related to the King of Prussia soon to become the Emperor of Germany. Meanwhile, in Bucharest, a crowd of insurgents set fire to the city hall throwing the archives in the Dambovita River. As Minister of the Interior General Florescu ordered the troops to fire on the instigators--there were 20 casualties and many arrests. He also informed the Prince on the importance of immediately returning to Bucharest from Ems.

Prince Cuza immediately complied. Instead of repression the Prince decided to placate the populace and issued an amnesty. Needless to say both General Florescu and General Manu who had given orders to fire on the crowd were dismissed to calm things down. The sacrifice of Florescu, the man who alone could have swayed the army and protected the Prince, was considered a fatal mistake on Cuza's part, since it simply encouraged the opposition to take advantage of the Prince's weakness. A number of army officers in alliance with the liberal coalition stole into the Prince's palace in Bucharest at night and at gunpoint forced Cuza, his wife Elena and his mistress Maria Obrenovic to leave the country into exile on February 11, 1866. This also signified the end of General Florescu's initial career as Cuza's army organizer.

---

[36]Cuza, "Florescu and Army Reform," in War and Society in East Central Europe. *The East European Quarterly*, New York 1985.

CHAPTER IV

THE ROMANIAN ARMY'S PREPARATIONS FOR THE WAR OF INDEPENDENCE DURING THE RULE OF PRINCE CAROL I OF HOHENZOLLERN

In the spring of 1866, Carol I of Hohenzollern-Sigmaringen was crowned prince on the throne of Romania. The beginning of his rule was marked by opposition among officers still loyal to Cuza who had achieved the Union of the Principalities. Seven colonels, seven lieutenant-colonels, eleven majors, thirty-eight captains, thirty-nine lieutenants and thirty-eight second lieutenants led by the Generals Ioan Emanoil Florescu and Savel Manu drew up and signed a collective petition which requested an official examination and punishment of the officers who had broken their oath of allegiance. Prince Carol invoked the importance of military discipline and ignored the issue.[1]

The supreme interests of the Romanian State to preserve its national sovereignty, as well as the necessity of completing the organization and training of the army, undoubtedly explains why the new regime appreciated General Ioan Emanoil Florescu's qualities of organizer and military legislator. Consequently, after some years of reflection Prince Carol decided to offer the all important office of Minister of War to General Florescu in 1871 and became, in turn, one of his closest collaborators. The years 1866-1871 were indeed difficult for General Florescu who had retired from public life. On political grounds he was attacked by leading liberal politicians among them D. A. Sturdza, who accused him of having broken the law during his tenure of office under Prince Cuza. Florescu was also deeply affected by the reverses of the French army during the 1870-1871 Franco Prussian war ending with the abject surrender of his friend and protector Napoleon III at Sedan, a prisoner of the King of Prussia William I Hohenzollern the future Emperor of Germany (1871-1888). On a personal level Florescu was deeply saddened by the death of his first wife Ecaterina Bibescu. His loyalty towards former Prince Cuza remained steadfast and is proven by continuing correspondence with the prince to his various palaces in exile in Paris, Vienna, Florence, and finally, Heidelberg where Cuza died on May 15, 1873. Florescu, of course, disapproved of Cuza's disorderly private life with his mistress Maria Obrenovici and his wife Elena, who took care of his illegitimate children.[2] The General maintained

---

[1] Constantin C. Giurescu, *Viata si opera lui Cuza Voda...*, pages 437-438.

[2] Radu R. Florescu, *Elena Cuza dincolo de legenda*, in, "*Magazin Istoric*," January 1998.

correspondence with Elena after Cuza's death and later congratulated the Princess for her hospital work in Jassy.

In the meantime the radical liberal forces had initiated a harsh campaign to discredit the Prince and remove him from the throne.[3] C. A. Rosetti had fled to France and contacted republican circles in Tours. His example was followed by others who enrolled in the French army. In August 1870 a Republican movement led by Major Candianu Popescu had occurred in Ploesti. Rebellions of the kind also began in Bucharest on March 10, 1871 when the German Colony celebrated the birthday of Emperor William I and Germany's victory over France. The guests of the German Consul von Radowitz were attacked and injured. This initiative was considered at least inappropriate in a country with obvious Francophile sympathies. The intervention of infantry and cavalry troops was necessary to calm things down. As we can see prince Charles' position had become very difficult in the first months of 1871 when the German newspaper *Augsburger Allgemeine Zeitung* published a letter disclosing the Prince's intention to abdicate.[4]

In the meantime another scandal erupted in Bucharest. In his endeavor to establish a railroad company Prince Carol conceded the affair to a German capitalist named Strousberg who, in turn, placed it in the hands of an unscrupulous financier called Ambronn and a banker Jacques who represented the Romanian state. Heated debates took place in the Romanian Parliament over their financial malversations, deputies accusing the Ghica-Kogalniceanu government of complicity. Although opposed to the government it was characteristic of General Florescu's sentiment of fair play to defend the ministry of any implication in the scandal.[5] In the end only commissary Ambronn and banker Jacques were sued. In the meantime Florescu supported the nomination of former Prince Cuza as a suitable candidate for the Mehedinti District and later for the City Council of Turnu-Severin, all to no avail.

A new conservative government under the leadership of Lascar Catargiu took over the government in 1871, the longest period of moderate conservative rule which prevailed in the early period of Prince Carol's reign from 1871-1875.[6] It was formed during a most delicate period, with the army patrolling the streets of Bucharest to preserve order.

General Florescu's nomination as Minister of War in the Catargiu government in 1871 came as a surprise as he had been essentially acknowledged as Prince Cuza's man. His acceptance of that post represented the longest incumbency in that office in the history of modern

---

[3] Dan Berindei, editor, *Istoria romanilor…*, vol. VII, t. 1, Bucharest, 2003, pages 5-9.

[4] *Istoria Romaniei*, vol IV, pages 556-557.

[5] *Generalul Florescu…*, page 34; Ion E Batali, *Generalul Florescu – un precursor al armatei romane moderne*, page 77.

[6] Dimitrie Costescu, *Fazele ministeriale in Romania*, Bucharest, 1936, pages 57-65.

Romania. Prince Carol attempted to explain his choice of Florescu in his Memoirs, in a letter dated March 14/26: "General Florescu is a dynamic man whose attractive martial looks exercise a fascination which is doubled by his elegant manners. He is a good musician, very touched by beauty in all forms. He loves his work and has initiative and pride." The following month Prince Carol specified in a letter dated April 17/29, 1872, and addressed to his father: "General Florescu was criticized in 1866 because he was loyal to Cuza. The officers who were loyal to Cuza are precisely the ones I can count on because they were faithful to a principle and not a person."[7]

During this second period of Florescu's tenure a totally different situation than the one during Cuza's rule existed. In the previous period, the correspondence between Florescu and Cuza showed that almost without exception the General's suggestions were approved by the Prince, because the latter did not have the skills of a man of war. In the person of Prince Carol, Florescu was dealing with an officer who had a very first rate military training in the Prussian army where he had completed his military service as an artillery lieutenant in an elite regiment in 1857.[8] He was an admirer of Helmut von Moltke, a great general who had noticed the Prince's talents. Carol had participated in the war between Prussia and Denmark in 1864. Earlier he was sent as an observer of French armies in the colonial wars in Algeria where he became convinced of the superiority of the Prussian army. It was easy for General Florescu himself, a good military man, to recognize a kindred talent in another. On the other hand Prince Carol needed Florescu's experience because only he knew of the reforms initiated during Cuza's rule. Even though Prince Carol was loyal to Germany his native country, gradually a mutual esteem developed between these two professional soldiers who shared the same ideal, namely, completing the organization of the Romanian army begun under Prince Cuza.[9] Nonetheless in the intimacy of Florescu's family circle, Prince Carol was always referred to as "The German" who wished to organize the Romanian army on the Prussian model – on the advice of the Prince's chief counselor Lieutenant-Colonel von Krenski.

Florescu, on the other hand, was determined to maintain French army officers on his staff as well as Romanians who had done their

[7] In the same letter of the Prince to his father (April 17-29, 1872) he also stated: "The present minister of War, General Florescu, was even from Cuza's period and particularly after February 11 the target of the red party that had denigrated him during the army organization. He started by making the mistake to have followed entirely the French model, but he has abandoned this idea today. All I can say is that I am very pleased with him and that he supports all my wishes." – Stelian Neagoe, ed., *Memoriile regelui Carol al Romaniei*, Bucharest, 1995, vol. III, page 185.

[8] R. W. Seton-Watson, *History of the Romanians*, Oxford, 1934, page 314.

[9] It should be remembered that prince Charles also had French blood in his veins by way of his grandmother General Murat's granddaughter.

schooling in France. Though he found it hard to accept such nominations, Prince Carol in the end complied. A good example to illustrate Florescu's confirmed sympathy for France was the case of second lieutenant Alexandru Vidrescu an officer who studied at St. Cyr in Paris. Caught by the Franco-Prussian war of 1870-71, he decided to enroll in the French army as a second lieutenant. Aware of the Prince's pro-German sympathy, General Florescu insisted on re-enlisting the young man in the Romanian army. His request was eventually approved by Prince Carol--a case similar to that of others, which proved that many of Florescu's protégés who had been trained in France succeeded in rebuilding their career in the country.[10] Florescu always recognized the talent of the French and other officers who had served Cuza's army. He continued using their services and, if need be, rewarded them by granting Romanian citizenship. This was the case of Lieutenant Colonel Henric Herkt of Flemish origin who had rendered invaluable services. Florescu appealed to the Romanian Senate to grant him the right of citizenship. During a session which took place in the Senate on February, 1872, the General declared, "I keep asking myself why Mr. Herck is not a Romanian citizen...he always considered himself a Romanian." This request was eventually granted.[11]

The philosophy underlining Florescu's second tenure at the War Office was in part influenced by study of the Prussian military machine that had revolutionized modern warfare during the Six Weeks War against Austria in 1866 and the Franco-Prussian War in 1870-71. These campaigns reinforced Florescu's conviction that henceforth victory favored well schooled recruits such as a trained reserve force like the Prussian Landwehr. In his eyes discipline and military education went hand in hand with universal conscription.[12] As a conservative Florescu boasted that the creation of such an army required placing the traditional concept of the "nation in arms" within the context of modern warfare. All this would be accomplished in accordance with the general's "peu a peu" approach by improving upon existing military legislation such as the army laws of 1868 with the new measures he introduced in Parliament in 1872-1874, and 1876.[13]

In many ways the most interesting aspect of Florescu's work centered upon the 1872 and 1874 laws concerning the "territorials" which

---

[10] "*Monitorul Oficial*" (the Senate's debates), no. 16, 1872, pages 318-319. The main sources for this period are "*Monitorul Oficial*," "*Monitorul Oastei*" and *The Memoirs of King Carol I.*

[11] "*Monitorul Oficial*" (the Senate's debates), 1871-1872, pages 506-507.

[12] M.O., vol. IX, 1872, no. 25, pages 409-410.

[13] General Florescu explained that the reserves' periodic mobilization has the purpose to "keep them abreast of the changes which might occur during the period of their staying home" – "*Monitorul Oficial*" (the Senate's debates), 1874, Session of March 2, pages 432-434. The importance of the territorial army increased; the reserves were called up for 15 days a year.

were given a new identity and importance. The dorobanti were now mounted, given new uniforms and hence renamed calarasi. The former graniceri (frontier guards) were advanced to the exalted status of dorobanti. The militias organized in battalions and squadrons were attached to either dorobanti or calarasi units, and hence, became part of the territorials and were trained by professional army officers. Over the years this force became indistinguishable from the permanent army of 30,000 troops. The militia reserve would constitute one-third of the whole army during the War of Independence. Young men aged 21-37 would enlist by rotations with one-quarter of their four years under arms and the balance in reserve. The reserves were summoned for 15 days during the autumn maneuvers to keep abreast of the latest military techniques and weaponry (Law of 1874). Proud of the accomplishment of being able to mobilize great numbers of men with little cost to the state, Florescu boasted (January 13, 1876): "We possess a territorial army organized as none other, since we were able to assemble four times the number of trained men that the yearly allocations provide for. This unique tradition has won the admiration of specialists from other nations."

Promotion by merit, a military hierarchy, compulsory military service for all able-bodied 21-year-olds (thus doing away with demoralizing system of conscription by lot, where wealthy young men purchased peasant recruits to serve in their place), a law for the development of a general staff and a consultative war council, a one year officer school, the enactment of a penal code--all bore Florescu's imprimatur between 1873-1876.[14]

He then tackled the separate army units. By adding four brigades of calarasi territorials to the permanent regiments now renamed rosiori, resplendent in their scarlet red tunics, Florescu laid himself open to the charge of having a top-heavy cavalry--a total of eight squadrons of rosiori and 32 of calarasi, not really required by the needs of the infantry, very much the dominant arm in the post-Crimean period.[15] The founder of Bibescu's artillery, Florescu also enhanced the role of that arm. In 1872 a battery of artillery was attached to each regiment of the line. The law of 1874 added two batteries, constituting the "territorial artillery," to the newly founded dorobanti and graniceri (40 [16] officers, 752 men, and 558 horses). These were composed of militiamen and firemen, and trained by professional army officers. The artillery pieces were purchased in France, Austria and Belgium, but significantly, also in Germany, where Florescu obtained the latest 1870 78- and 87-mm caliber model Krupp steel-barreled

[14] "*Monitorul Oficial*" (the Senate's debates), 8174, Session of March 2, pages 432-434. The appendix of the law increased the importance of the territorial army. General Radu Rosetti, *Partea luata de armata romana in razboiul din 1877-1878*, Bucharest, 1926, pages 12-13, also see M.O., pages 412-414, M.O., vol. IV, 1872, no. 19, pages 341-344.

[15] Major I. Popovici, *Armata romana*, page 297.

[16] General Ioan Emanoil Florescu, *Espunere de imbunatatirile cele mai insemnatoare in armata Principatelor Unite de la 24 ianuarie- 1 iunie 1860*, Bucharest, 1861.

cannons capable of firing projectiles with percussion fuses at great distance. Most of the heavy cannon for the defense of the Danubian bridgeheads, the field howitzers of older vintage, the famous 1872 Christophe-Montigny "mitrailleuse" mounted on a carriage, and the revolvers issued to officers and rank and file were of French design, though the latter were perfected by Captain Vasile Buescu, Director of the Bucharest Arsenal.

Judging from Parliamentary records in *Monitorul Oficial* Florescu did not receive the satisfaction of seeing his army reach the numbers and qualitative standards of excellence for which he had set his goals, for lack of funds. His Parliamentary speeches, delivered in short clipped sentences, devoid of rhetorical flourish, failed to convince his liberal foes to increase military budgets.[17] In 1872, 17,000,000 leis were asked for the army, 8,000,000 leis in 1874 for barracks and road construction, another 4,000,000 more for weapons, munitions, ambulances and other war material. Since these sums proved insufficient Florescu asked for an additional loan of 8,000,000 francs in Paris to defray the costs of blankets, uniforms, and the like. In 1876, 4,000,000 lei was spent for the procurement of additional weaponry and ambulances. "How can you command respect in the barracks," he pleaded on one occasion, "when officers and sergeant majors are compelled to share cramped quarters?"[18] Because of lack of money, rifles for the infantry and munitions were purchased at random at minimum cost: second-hand French "chassepots" captured by the Prussians in 1870-71, the German Dreyse and the Russian Krnk (15.45mm rifles) with insufficient cartridges to match the various models – all inferior to the Henry Winchesters available to the Turks. Though a law providing for Florescu's War Academy was passed in 1872, it was only founded 16 years later. The corps of engineers had to be reduced from two battalions to one, even though specialized services of pontooners, telegraphers and sappers were set up. Merely getting the necessary appropriations for the yearly contingents from 1872 to 1876, which varied from 12,000 to 18,000 men was a *tour de force*. Passing to the offensive, Florescu's detractors accused him of ordering useless equipment in excess of needs and diverting resources and funds for personal ends. Most of his Parliamentary opponents were civilians who did not understand the military needs of a professional soldier on the eve of a major conflict. When new recruits were needed in 1872, deputies complained that their lands went uncultivated because of lack of hands. They denounced General Florescu as "belligerent" in calling the military contingent under arms during the harvest period in *"order to start a war"* to secure state independence. It was with a note of irony that a deputy Colonel Lacusteanu interrupted Florescu making a speech in the Senate: *"Whom do we make a war against? Is it the government's intention to do that?"* Florescu responded with dignity and patriotism: *"The words of*

[17] *Studii si pregatiri militare*, Bucharest, 1878.
[18] "*Monitorul Oficial*," no. 119, June 2/14, 1876, page 29.

honorable Colonel Lacusteanu make me rather sad because anyone who wishes for his country to exist will have to consider a reasonable and economical army [...] with daily needs which require the support of this law. He will have to do that before thinking about all the other serious reasons which the honorable Mr. Lacusteanu does not approve. Gentlemen Senators, you will see that we shall be forced to start a war. Did he tell you who we shall fight against? And do you know why Mr. Lacusteanu asks this question? Because that day has not yet arrived. When it does, do you want it to find us unprepared?"[19]

Florescu was never able to prove his skills as a commander in war, though he discussed military matters with Prussian officers in Prince Charles's entourage such as Lieutenant Colonel Von Krenski, attended the yearly maneuvers of major foreign armies (those of the Prussian Army near Hanover in 1874, the Russian Army in 1876 near St. Petersburg), and conversed with foreign staff officers.[20] Neither he nor Prince Charles kept completely up to date with the most recent strategy or tactics. Convinced of General Cantilli's truism that the importance of the infantry is related to the perfection of its fire power, Florescu saw an offensive prepared in the classical manner by long-range artillery fire. The battalions would then advance in column formation, protected by "mitrailleurs" on the flanks.[21] Closer range enemy positions would be further "softened" by machine gunners and grenade throwers, allowing the main body of the infantry and its reserves to reach the vanguard enemy positions. At that point, the artillery is utilized, to allow for the final infantry or cavalry charge.[22] Should the enemy falter, the attack must be pursued with vigor in "square formation," while the surviving skirmishers would cover the retreat, moving from flank to the center, to delay pursuit. If the enemy cavalry charges the retreating infantry must resort to bayonets. Meanwhile, the artillery should continue intense fire until such time as the army was able to regroup to more advantageous positions. Florescu placed great reliance on the vanatori, fighting in small units showing great initiatives because of their unusual training and less centralized command.[23]

The yearly maneuvers which took place in the various parts of the country each autumn from 1872 to 1876 were aimed principally at mobilizing the army, simulating actual conditions of warfare to test the tactics and strategy prepared by the General Staff. In 1872 these took place

---

[19] "*Monitorul Oficial at Romaniei*," extraordinary session, 1871-1872, pages 540-554.

[20] *Generalul Florescu*, The Political Library, page 127, (no author).

[21] *Generalul Ioan Emanoil Florescu, "Studii si pregatiri militare"*, page 15.

[22] C. Cazanisteanu, G. Tudor, *Armata romana in preajma razboiului,* in the volume *Romania in Razboiul de Independenta*; I. Ghitu, *Evolutia instruirii si a tacticei infanteriei romane de la 1831 la 1931*, in "Revista infanteriei," year XXXV, no. 350, 1931, page 132.

[23] H. Herkt, *Modificarea in tactica artileriei de camp, ca consecinta a perfectionarii armelor de foc portative si a materialelor artileriei de camp.* Georgescu Printing House, Buzau, 1877, page 8.

for 15 days on the line of the Arges River with 11,000 participating. In the words of a correspondent: "It was the first time that an army mobilized from every region of the country and executed a maneuver covering a 120 square kilometer area." In 1874, 18,000 soldiers, including territorials, took part in the practice. Florescu wrote: *"The mobilization of the troops for exercises and maneuvers this year has taken greater importance than during the preceding years because of the deployment of the territorials (the dorobanti and graniceri) increasing the permanent army to four regiments, thus enabling us to form the major units which would be used in actual condition of warfare."*[24] The efficiency in the execution won general praise from all the military observers present. Characteristic was the remark of the Turkish military attaché, who turning to the admiring British colleague Colonel John Morris stated: *"It would be in Turkey's interest to grant independence to Romania and then form an alliance with that country."* In a circular dated November 23, 1874, addressed to the commanding officers of the territorials, Florescu stated: *"This year virtually all the representatives of the European armies attended our maneuvers. I believe I can state that our army has made an excellent impression on all foreign observers. I am convinced that you will understand the positive consequences of this great event."*[25] Though Romania remained neutral during the Serbo-Montenegrin conflict with Turkey (June-September 1, 1875) in accordance with the Red Cross convention that was signed at Geneva (November 30, 1874), Florescu sent an ambulance corps under Charles Davila to Serbia, to care for some 6,800 wounded, many of those lives were saved.[26]

On 27 April 1875 Ion Bratianu asked for a meeting with Prince Carol in an attempt to remove the Conservative government from office--the latter had survived five years even though criticized in the Senate and Chamber. It had also lost prestige due to the resignation of a number of prominent cabinet members such as Vasile Boerescu, Minister of Public Instruction; Gheorghe Cantacuzino, Minister of Finance; and others. After a vote of censure in the Senate indirectly aimed at Florescu, the moderates would normally have been asked by the Prince to form a new coalition including some moderate liberal politicians under the premiership of Manolache Costache Epureanu. However, the Prince was not easily swayed to remove a conservative grouping to which he had become accustomed; above all, he needed a strong military man such as Florescu at the War Office at the time of the eruption of the Bosnia-Herzegovian crisis. In fact, the change of Prime Ministership rebounded in Florescu's favor who

[24] "*Monitorul Oficial*," vol. II, 1872, no. 28, pages 370-376.
[25] "The circular concerning the autumn calling up of July 1874," *The State Archives*, Bucharest, package 416/1874, file 12, p. 279. Also see, *"Monitorul Oficial,"* vol. XII, 1875, no. 28, page 483; for the circular concerning the autumn mobilization in 1874, *The State Archives*, Bucharest, the Ministry of War, package 416, file 12, p. 279.
[26] Maria Radovici, *Ajutorul acordat Serbiei in anul 1876 de catre ambulanta societatii de Cruce Rosie din Romania*, in "SMMM, MMC," 1876, pages 79-80.

replaced Lascar Catargiu in April 1876 while preserving the position of Minister of War. Carol still deemed him the most able politician to weather the Eastern crisis.

The governing program which the General presented to Parliament on April 15, 1876, though in essence favoring Russia's initiatives in favor of her Slavic neighbors, he was well aware of the fact that Romania was *de jure* still a vassal of the Sultan and thus favored a policy of strict neutralilty. Unfortunately, the General failed to convince the majority in the House of Parliament, as his opponents engineered *"a coup"* to force the King to dismiss this new government. The coup was organized at the home of a well known Englishman Sir Steven Lakeman, an Englishman, who had converted to Islam under the name of Mazar Pacha; hence the formation of a new government known as "the Mazar Pacha coalition." The anti-Florescu plotters, Manolache Costache Epureanu, Ion Bratianu, Mihail Kogalniceau – both liberals and conservatives finally succeeded in persuading the Prince to dismiss the Florescu government, a very personal blow to the General in itself. The anti-Florescu movement was, however, far from over. Indeed, the General, as well as members of the previous conservative government of Catargiu, was dragged into an ugly conspiracy of character assassination. On July 10/22, 1876 one of Florescu's enemies Nicolae Fleva, a member of Parliament, introduced a motion signed by 60 deputies requesting that the former members of the conservative government be indicted for having "violated the constitution, wasted public funds and abused their power." The motion was in the first instance directed against General Florescu. The irony of it all was that it was one of General Florescu's former students, Colonel Gheorghe Slaniceanu, now Minister of War, who played a most important role in the denunciation of his peer. The Colonel accused the General of having acquired military hardware, arms and munitions well in excess of the needs of the army. In response, the General took full responsibility for all his army requests, *"I am,"* he stated, *"the only one responsible for my actions and only regret that I was not able to do more for an institution which I considered most useful to our country in the service of which I placed all my efforts and devotion."*[27] Fortunately, the affair did not proceed much further as more responsible political

[27] Stelian Neagoe, ed., Memoriile Regelui Carol al Romaniei, vol. III, page 16: "The situation of the government is very unstable because of the budget. The Chambers are revolted because of the deficit which has been hidden up to now [...] The commission in charge of the budget intends to reduce the budget of the Ministry of War, but Minister Florescu strongly protests against the oriental complications which become more and more threatening." Balaceanu tells the Prince on behalf of Bratianu that the throne will be in danger if he does not change the government immediately. The Prince accepts the resignation of the Catargiu government with regret. General Florescu advises Prince Carol to appoint the former senator C. Bosianu in charge with the framing of the constitution of the cabinet. Prince Carol is in a very difficult situation as he does not want to appoint a civilian at the head of the Ministry of War.

personalities such as Epureanu and Kogalniceanu downed the motion of censure by an overwhelming majority. Ion Bratianu was appointed by Carol as the new Prime Minister (June 23, 1876). Nonetheless, the slanderous campaign against the General continued by way of the press and certain radical pamphlets for another year. Their main aim was to keep the General out of power. Prince Carol disapproved of this disparaging campaign against his former minister and friend. He made a point of it by inviting Florescu to a reception which he gave at the palace in honor of the newly appointed Russian Consul General Baron Dmitri Fiodorovici Stuart to the consternation of the government in power. Though elected to a parliamentary seat in the Romanati district, Florescu's enemies prevent him from occupying it on a technicality though in the end the General was elected to the Senate and in turn became President of that body.[28]

By far the most cruel revenge was soon to follow at the outbreak of the Russo Turkish conflict of 1877-78 when Bratianu instead of naming Florescu, who had built the Romanian army as Commander in Chief, appointed Brigadier General Alexander Cernat in his stead until Csar Nicholas II asked Prince Charles himself to take command of the joint Romanian-Russian forces when the Russians ran into difficulties in Bulgaria. The government refused Florescu any command appointment on the front, a most humiliating punishment. He was compelled to follow the outcome of a conflict he had long prepared for and predicted as an embittered armchair critic, confined to his house in Bucharest.

Proud of the accomplishment "of his children" during the Bulgarian campaign, Florescu thought that independence could equally have been secured without the heavy losses incurred helping the Russians capture Plevna. In a pamphlet: *A Few Words Upon the Entry of the Troops in Action* (Bucharest, 1877), he cited the example of the role of the Piedmontese Army during the Crimean War, and true to his defensive thinking, he wrote that only a small token force of 15,000 should have been sent across the Danube while the bulk of the army should have been located on defensive fortifications he had long recognized along the Danube. The strategy might have precluded the loss of Bassarabia, for which he held Ion Bratianu responsible. No matter the price (the cession of S. Bessarabia in 1878 at the Congress of Berlin), Romania had achieved its independence. As he watched the proud veterans return to Bucharest on October 8, 1878 he turned to a friend and told him with tears in his eyes, "It is the most beautiful day of my life."

In spite of all the accusations brought by his enemies against him, most of Florescu's contemporaries continued to appreciate his merits and contributions to this victorious army. In the newspaper *Timpul* of April 20, 1876, an officer printed an article entitled, "The Romanian Army in 1876"

[28] I. Batalli, *Generalul Ioan Em. Florescu – un precursor al armatei romane moderne*, in "EMMM," Bucharest, 1976, page 75.

which emphasized the important part played by the General in the army endowment. “I have often written that the army has made progress every year and its structure has become stronger than before 1870. In this five year period we all have seen it well trained, well equipped and very well disciplined. The maneuvers performed during this time proved they were admired by all the foreigners who came here precisely to see them. Whom do we have to show our gratitude to and who should take the credit of this capacity and effort if not my honorable comrade-in-arms and leader of the army, division General Ioan Emanoil Florescu.”

But the most beautiful tribute brought to General Florescu belongs to one of the greatest Romanian poets, Vasile Alecsandri, a devoted friend, who wrote a poem in his honor which was published in *Timpul* on February 9, 1878.[29]

When we were young, Florescu, my friend
When every hope was dying and came to life again
A great ideal and a noble wish we shared
To deliver Romania from its sad despair.

All with one consciousness and close-knit in one thought
In sacrifice, in virtue, in brotherhood we joined
All together the sacred battalion we enrolled
And in each of us an ardent wish burgeoned:
I hoped to praise in songs our ancestors’ great story
You hoped to bring to life our army’s daring glory.
A secret wish, a hopeful dream, a splendid thought in vain
A brave and glorious desire, fruit of our youth’s strain?

And thus our pure soul which wandered in the sky
The very future touched when it began to fly.
And every hard obstacle and terrifying specter
Would fade just like the night under the sun’s shelter.

By hard work and long years of diligence
Your strong belief has born the fruits of perseverance.
A stately and proud army comes to life today
The very future touched when I began to fly.
And every hard obstacle and terrifying specter
Would fade just like the light under the sun’s shelter.

[29] Poem addressed to General Florescu, inserted in the newspaper *Timpul* and dated January 4th, 1878.

General Ioan Emanoil Florescu

By hard work and long years of diligence
Your strong belief has born the fruits of perseverance.
A stately and proud army comes to life today
And it is meant to surpass what the world may say
It throws itself in fire and conquers even more
For the glorious feats of the times of yore.
And just like me you felt so proud at their sight
And still you wore so much bitterness in your heart
When seeing our soldiers go forward in pride
Forgetting their father and leaving him behind.

On the remote fields of death we looked in despair
To seek for the light of your old spear
The whole army increased the power of its fire
And asked to hear your voice in the cannons' roar.
Because you made this army so lively, brave and young
Under the rules of Cuza and that of King Carol,
You should have had the honor to lead us in the battle
As you are the organizer, the man who made it happen.

Yet, victim of oppression so vengeful and so blind
They left you like a villain, they left you all behind!

You, a villain! Good Lord, since when has the daylight worn
The same name the dark night was given in this world?
And since what time a villain is the man
Who dedicates his life for his country's fame?
And since what time the villain is the soldier
Who bravely sacrifices for his country's honor?
And since what time a villain is the leader
Who, despite the conditions, defends his flag and vision?

My friend be at rest and comfort your grief…
In every soldier today find your relief,
Because every Romanian knows and feels inside
That the ancestors' sword received with you more light.
And when you watch the flag with your eyes amazed
The living colors quiver in a majestic wave.

CHAPTER V

IOAN EMANOIL FLORESCU: INSTRUCTOR AND ORGANIZER OF MILITARY EDUCATION

General Florescu's role as an army instructor goes beyond pure military affairs. He was a cultured man who extensively studied the classics, literature, history and music at St. Sava, one of the best Romanian lyceums of the period in Bucharest. He also had a scientific mind and excelled at physics, chemistry and mathematics. An accomplished linguist he spoke French with perfection and translated a number of plays he wrote as a young man in that language. Though not a great orator, his parliamentary speeches are worth reading in the *Army Monitor*, which he founded, as well as the *Military Observer*. Toward the end of his life, he enjoyed lecturing to a variety of audiences both academic, and open to the public at large such as the "Society for the Education of the Romanian People. However, his first love remained the education of the military.

The great historian and future forty-eighter Nicolae Balcescu recognized Florescu's talents at an early age and dedicated one of his works entitled "*The Power of the Army and Military Since the Foundation of the Wallachian Principality*" to the future General. Drawing attention to the illiteracy of the rank and file and the lack of culture of the Officerial Corps, taught Florescu the most important lesson: namely, that the barracks must serve as a primary school for soldiers beginning with basic reading and writing.[1]

During the early years of the Russian sponsored Organic Statutes, Prince Alexander Ghica one of Florescu's early patrons instructed the Minister of Education Petrache Poenaru to establish a kind of school for both infantry and cavalry in every army barrack in Bucharest. General Florescu, then a young officer showed interest in the curriculum and also liked the idea of introducing gymnastics and swimming classes in accordance with his lifetime motto: "mens sana in corpore sano."

An aide to Prince Gheorghe Bibescu and with the rank of Colonel, Florescu was named member of a commission entrusted with the task of establishing a school to prepare the Princes' Officerial Corps with focus on courses of tactics and strategy (February 1847). In a sense this marked the beginnings of Romania's military education.[2] The Wallachian Assembly approved the necessary funds: 16,000 leis for books, 10,000 leis for hygiene and 30,000 leis for the salary of teachers. These humble beginnings were

---

[1]Maria Stan, Contributii la cunoasterea istoriei invatamantului militar din Bucurestit in secolul at XIX - lea, in "Muzeul militar central," no. 6, 1973, page 129.

[2]Cornelia Bodea, Paul Cernovodeanu, *Primele scoli ostasesti din Tara Romaneasca*, 1838-1840, in "Studii si articole de istorie," volume VIII, Bucharest, 1966, pages 105-116; M.O. (Wallachia), year I, no. 3, February 20, page 37.

soon interrupted with the outbreak of the revolution of 1848 when the school ceased to function. A more ambitious school reopened in 1849 under the rule of Prince Stirbey. General Florescu, Colonel Ioan Voinescu and the mathematician Dimitri Pavlide were in charge of choosing an appropriate building, deciding upon the number of students and faculty, set entry standards and curriculum.[3] Another order signed by Prince Barbu Stirbey (August 1856) encouraged the involvement of all officers who wished to dedicate themselves to a military career. In 1857, fencing and gymnastics classes were added to the syllabus as well as geography, arithmetic, history, calligraphy and foreign languages (French and German) classes. Apart from Florescu, among the faculty were notable personalities such as Alexandru Orascu and Carol Davila, the future general and head of the Sanitary Corps.[4]

Finally the law for the establishment of a unified army was published in Monitorul Oastei on May 26, 1860. Article I stipulated that "the training exercise and discipline of the army of the United Principalities, the setting up of a General Staff, the administration and accountancy, will from this point onwards be standardized. The second article requested that the training of the army be in charge of certain "model detachments" which existed in all branches of the services from both Principalities which will be discussed in some detail. Apart from General Florescu, General Adrian temporarily the head of the Wallachian army also played an important role in drafting the document.[5]

Another provisional military school began functioning in Iasi in 1856. With the Union of the two Principalities under Prince Cuza in 1859, Florescu wrote: "These army barracks became genuine schools where trainees not only completed their education, but also where we can touch their hearts by encouraging love of fatherland."

Florescu focused on that theme in innumerable lectures delivered in the course of his career. One of his most popular pamphlets was entitled: "*The Military Institution Based on Education.*" He stated, "The military institution which must defend the state's independence can only progress by means of education. Words such as 'compulsory education' written in the constitution should cease to be fiction." He aimed his remarks particularly at the minority of military men from the rural areas still illiterate. The General placed much emphasis on these initial elementary stages in all military school and made it his constant priority. Thus, elementary textbooks were placed at the soldier's disposal. An Order of the Day (March

[3]Under the caption: "various things about the military school," Maria Stan, "contribut ie la cunoasterea invatamantului military in Secolul at XIX lea" in *Studii Si materiale de muzeografie si istorie militara*. Central Military Muzeum, no. 6, p. 137-139.

[4]"Cu privire la masurile luate de Alexandru Ioan Cuza in anii 1859-1861 pentru unificarea si organizarea armalei" *Studii si materiale di Museografie* si Istorie militara, Central Military Museum, no. 6-5 pages, 127-141.

[5]Monitorul Oastei (Wallachie) May 26, 1860.

20, 1860) decreed that elementary education be introduced in every military unit. Physical education which the General termed "exercises for the body" also was introduced.

Moved by Florescu, Lieutenant E. U. Pencovici drew up a textbook for all future Army Schools in 1860 (reprinted in 1863). The General expressed his appreciation of the young officer's works" "I have seen the author's hard work in completing this text in record time. It has been approved for the entire army of the United Principalities and 10,000 copies will be printed by the Ministry of War.[6]

To further encourage "patriotism" and love of country, Florescu asked his good friend the poet Vasile Alecsandru to contribute to army education. The poet complied and wrote a number of poems and other words extolling the heroism of the Romanian army in the course of its past history.

To further encourage patriotism and love of country Florescu appealed to a number of writers and poets to extol the heroism of the Romanian army in the course of its history. Among them was of course Florescu's lifelong friend Vasile Alecsandri who composed "Sobieski and his Troops," modeled on one of Negruzzi's poems. Other folk ballads followed glorifying past Romanian leaders such as the biography of Stefan the Great and Mihai the Brave describing their various victories where Romanians fought to defend their soil against Poles, Turks, and Hapsburg Imperialists to preserve their national identity. One of the writings included in the text was written by General Florescu himself entitled: "The Soldier's Duty."[7]

In his textbook Lieutenant Pencovici also showed interest in the soldier's musical education. General Florescu strongly believed in the importance of music in awakening the soldier's courage in battle, a factor which had inspired German, Scottish and Scandinavian armies in the course of their history. In this respect he was helped by his nephew Dumitru Florescu the 1848 revolutionary who had studied music in Paris under well-known professors at the time. He ranks as one of the great Romanian composers of the end of the 19th century. One of his works was *Hora Uniru* already alluded to written in 1859, following Prince Cuza's double election and was played during his official entrance in Bucharest. Dumitru Florescu remained one of the General's intimates until Cuza's abdication in 1866. Returning to Bucharest many years later, he established a music school and was one of the co-founders of the Bucharest Music Conservatory, as well as

---

[6]"Good officers are educated in schools[...], the Spartans and several ancient republics know this necessity and create military gymnasiums where the young men who are destined to a military career come to study." See "Monitorul Oastei (Tara Romaneasca)," no. 1, 1860, page 13.

[7]*Datoriile ostasului*, Bucharest, 1876.

one of its first teachers. This pioneer of Romanian music died in 1875, barely aged 48.

Besides *Hora lui Cuza*, among the military songs approved by General Florescu were: *The Song of Stefan the Great, The Song of Mihai the Brave, The Cavalry Marches, The Infantry Marches,* and *one entitled: Stefan the Great and his Hawks* all inspired by victorious campaigns meant to awaken sentiments of honor, patriotism and courage.

A few examples of these lyrics are pertinent:

"Steven Steven greatest prince
Nobody resembles him
But the glorious sun...Stefan greatest prince
Places his chest on the borders
Like a defensive wall...."
Or, Mihai the Brave:
"Have you ever heard of an Oltenian a Craiovean
Who defies the sultan?
Have you ever heard of a brave man?
Who is watching very carefully
When the country is in trouble
Have you ever heard of Mihai?
Who rides on seven horses
And makes the sultan cry?"
There was a "Cavalry March:"
"I am a Romanian green like an oak
I mock our enemies and I mock death
Long live my stallion
And let him carry me through fire.
As long as I hold my strong hand
On my gun
Nothing could threaten/My Romanian land."
And finally, the "Infantry March:"
"May the flag shine
Because we live for it
May the country live
Because we die for it!
Every soldier is ready to become part of Trajan's arm
For his country Romania!"

In a study pleading for the necessity of establishing an effective officer's school, Florescu stated "Good officers are educated in schools the foundations of which had been laid down for several years (during the Reglement period). We must bring our contribution to the development of these institutions among the most useful for our future. May God enable Romanian army officers give our country what it lacks most and compensate for the few number of soldiers in our army." He repeated speeches of the kind in the Romanian Senate during Prince Charles' reign pleading for ever larger budgets for officer school. His theme was invariably "knowledge is a good substitute for lack of numbers." By the end of March 1860 plans were finally presented to the Prince for the creation of a Military School in Bucharest for gifted officers.[8]

The length of the courses was initially established at five years, the number of students limited to 70, (though numbers could be increased at will). A quarter of the students received scholarships offered by the state: six full scholarships and twelve half-scholarships. The commanding officer and director of the school were appointed by the Prince on the recommendation of General Florescu.

The curriculum consisted of subjects considered necessary for a modern military instruction: higher mathematics, notions of geography, natural history, drawing, topography, geodesy, military art, fortifications, roads and bridges, engineering, military administration and legislation, special courses for cavalry and infantry, fencing exercises, gymnastics and swimming.

Article 4 of the Regulations stated that the school was subject to military norms and represented an autonomous institute under the authority of the Minister of War. To ensure high standards Florescu requested that all candidates attend a preparatory school and only those who passed this school at least with the rank of sergeant could apply for the Military School in Bucharest. Two additional Sergeant Schools were eventually added, one in Iasi and the other in Craiova.[9] All candidates were acceptable irrespective of social class.

Unfortunately, this principal officer's school only had a six year existence for on March 10/15, 1866, the building of the Bucharest Military School was destroyed by a fire. The school was temporarily moved to Iasi to a private dwelling which belonged to Ghica Deleanu in the Copou district. At last the new school took the name of *Preparatory School* or the *School for the Sons of Military Men.* In 1863 a school for Troop children was also founded in Iasi and merged with the Pedagogical Fencing, Engineering and Target Shooting Schools. When Prince Carol assumed power with Florescu at the War Office in 1872 the officer's school moved back to Bucharest in a new building.

Another interesting idea in army schooling for which Florescu was responsible was the creation of model regiments for all branches of military service. Each detachment consisted of elite officers, staff and even soldiers

---

[8]Report presented to Prince Cuza on March 30, 1860 (Resport No 1042).

[9]M.O. (Wallachia), an I, 1860, no. 11, April 2, pages 161; 163-165; I. Brezoianu, *quoted work*, page 229.

provided that they had served at least one year in the army. For infantry detachments the law stipulated the appointment of one battalion commander, a captain, and four officers; there was one captain and two non-commissioned officers for the Alpine troops. The cavalry detachment had one squadron commander, one lieutenant, three non-commissioned officers and one veterinarian. As for the artillery: one pedestrian battery commander, two non-commissioned officers, one riding battery commander, two non-commissioned officers and one pyrotechnician. The company of engineers had one engineering officer and four non-commissioned officers of the same arm. The military intendancy had a subintendant; the navy, one officer director and two non-commissioned officers.

Always a Francophile General Florescu persuaded parliament to keep a number of army officers in Romania during and even after the Cuza period to help train Romanian army officers within the country – most of the officers were French. As noted elsewhere the first to arrive in October 1861 was General Staff Officer Lieutenant Colonel Eugene Lamy who had fought with distinction in the Crimean War. A number of French officers were attached to his mission to help the Romanian infantry, cavalry, and artillery and accountancy departments. Usually one officer, one corporal, and a sergeant were allocated for each arm. Intendant Lecler, Artillery Captains Guerin and Bodin, as well as Engineering Captain Roussel and Eugene Lamy's brother also formed part of the French instruction team. Some of the same officers also taught at the officers' school.[10]

The greatest reward for an officer which Florescu had always encouraged was that of sending a young man abroad, particularly to France, a very costly affair which involved a small number of men because of budgetary restraints. The majority of Romanian students enrolled at the prestigious Cavalry School at St. Cyr and the Ecole Militaire. Others were sent to the Ecole Polytechnique in Paris, the Naval Academies at Brest and Toulon, medical schools and veterinary schools. Initially the number of officers sent to France was small. In 1860 only four cavalry officers were attending St. Cyr. Six artillery and engineering students were at the Polytechnique School in Paris. However, over a period of time the numbers

[10]The French team, led by Lieutenant-Colonel Lamy was made up of the non-commissioned officers Grincourt and Chaber for the artillery, Roussin for the engineering unit, Captains Guerin and Bodin, and also the administration officers Mengel and Serveille. See Georgescu, Misiunea militara franceza, p. 173. The French military mission reorganized the army administration and accountancy; M. Dimitrescu, *Amintiri din Razboiul de Independenta*, Bucharest, 1893, page 7; E. Palanceanu, *Cu privire la masurile luate de Alexandru Ioan Cuza intre 1859-1861*, page 158; Marcel Emerit, *Une conversation entre l'empereur et Basile Alecsandri*, in "Revue Historique du Sud-Est Europeen," no. 7-9, 1928, pages 232; 236; Idem, *Le dossier de la premiere mission militaire francaise en Roumanie (1860-1866),* in "Revue Roumaine d'Histoire," no. 4, 1966, page 586.

increased and over sixty Romanian officers served as trainees in France at various times..

Military education also involved participation in maneuvers abroad. On May 29/31, 1860 Captain Lecca and Lieutenants Slaniceanu, Plesoianu and Boranescu were mentioned as participants in joint exercises with the French army in the camps of Chalons and Toulon. Young Odobescu was authorized to attend the courses and exercises of the Cavalry School in Saumur. On October 10, 1862, Iancu Alecsandri wrote to Baligot de Beyne, the Prince's secretary, that Davila's five "protégés" were registered at the Medical School in Paris. One of them, Nichita Andritoiu had the title of "Military Doctor Student." In April 1863, Iancu Alecsandri informed Baligot de Beybe that five Romanian students were attending the artillery school in Metz. Lieutenants Dabija and Berindei distinguished themselves the most.

A Romanian naval officer who excelled in his studies was the future Admiral Murgescu. He was awarded a 300 gold coin scholarship for "exceptional performance" at the Navy School in Brest.[11] There were some failures as well. On Florescu's request Gheorghe Cuza, the Prince's nephew, was initially accepted to attend courses at St. Cyr provided he took the entrance examination. Unfortunately, he was not up to the standards of the school, a source of some embarrassment.[12] To avoid such failures, Florescu thought at one time of establishing a Romanian College in Paris to keep an eye on Romanian trainees –a project which never succeeded. A few Romanian officers were sent in operational theatres of war as "observers" mostly in North Africa during the French and Spanish campaigns in Morocco. In an Order of the Day, addressed to the entire army, General Florescu wrote on that occasion: *"The Ministry of War thinks that it is very important for our army to have officers who should be acquainted with the administration and the command of an army on the battlefield. We also believe that this necessity could be fulfilled today, in the Moroccan war. Therefore, during the session of February 9, the Ministry presented a report which requested sending two officers in Morocco attached to the Spanish army."*[13]

Although France continued to be the principal destination of these officer trainees, Florescu admitted that some completed their military education in other countries as well, among them were officers who participated in the Franco-Italian conflict with Austria in 1859 in the region of Gaeta and Messina. Letters written by the Italian General Goldini, the commander of the Italian troops and by the Minister of War, General Fanti to Florescu confirms the presence of these Romanian officers.

---

[11]Constantin Giurescu, *Viata si opera lui Cuza voda*, pages 422-424.

[12]Maria Georgescu, *Misiunea Militara Franceza...*,page 173.

[13]Order of the Day for the whole army, M.O. no. 30, 11 February 1860.

Military education during Florescu years at the War Office, also involved enlisted men obliged to read articles of a high scientific level in various military reviews. Among them were *Observatorul Militar al oastei Romane* (The Military Observer of the Roman Army) edited by two Lieutenants Grigore Lipoianu and Ion Voinescu and *Romania Militara* published in 1864. However, *Monitorul Oastei* (the army Monitor) founded by Florescu in 1859 became the most important official army publication during the whole period. Among many topics covered were Princely decrees, and Orders of the Day. The first issue published by the War Ministry was dated February 6, 1860 and was printed both in Bucharest and Iasi. Starting with the 22nd issue, *Monitorul Oastei* became the official army newspaper of the United Principalities. Apart from army affairs it also included articles on Romanian history, biography, diplomacy, details concerning the soldiers' daily routine, as well as encyclopedic-type articles. Typical headlines ran as follows: *"The Necessity of Military Schools; Fragments from the Historian Nicolae Balcescu; The Romanian Army Power; The Battle of Calugareni; A Brief History of the Military Establishment; The Importance of the Army Organizaton and the Soldier's Dignity; Cuza's Visit to Constantinople; The Role and the Use of Cavalry; and The Rifle as a Portable Weapon."*[14]

In the two chambers of the Romanian Parliament during Prince Cuza's and Prince Carol's reign there were few politicians who were knowledgeable in discussing army problems. This reality did not help in persuading Parliamentarians to increase army budgets. This applied particularly to a number of civilian Ministers who held the War Office in Florescu's absence--they simply did not have the requisite military experience. Even among men of culture, few politicians could write or speak knowledgeably about Romania's military past with Balcescu a notable exception. Florescu was in fact one of the very few who had a significant military education and in addition experience on the battlefront in Transylvania and during the Crimean War. He also became a self-styled military historian knowledgeable of the great battles of the world from antiquity onwards. He had studied carefully the campaigns of the French revolutionaries; those of the great Napoleon as well as Prussia' campaign against Austria and France. An interesting study on military history was entitled, *The Difference Between Ancient or Modern Armies*, published from a speech in the Romanian Senate in 1890. Florescu's first published work was a translation of *"A Soldier's Duties,"* a study by the French Captain Rocquancourt who had been one of his instructors in Paris in a course on military art, which was used at the School of St. Cyr. He was sufficiently impressed by this introductory course to print it in full in 1876 on the eve of the War of Independence. In the foreword noting the difference between ancient and modern armies he remarked: *"I would like*

[14]General Florescu, Espunere de imbunatatirile cele mai insemnatoare, pages 12-20.

our officers to read it very carefully." "... knowledge absolutely necessary for a soldier... drawing, topography, statistics, artillery, fortifications, assault and the defense of towns, army administration and legislation, tactics and strategy, history, geography, mathematics, - these represent an introduction to more specialized knowledge. Nobody should ever think that we ask too much of our officers, because otherwise how could we ever entrust them with the lives of our citizens, the glory and the destiny of our country?" Also included were *"...ideas which concern the role of the soldiers' physical and tactical training, by marches, body exercises, the manning of weapons, and also the studying of certain battles."*[15]

This introduction ended with a quotation of an historian of Antiquity: "I am not satisfied with my soldiers being brave, I also want them to be honest!"[16] The last pages of the treaties emphasized the importance of civil behavior on the part of soldiers which transforms the army from an instrument of repression into an institution of good moral standards, correct manners and good education.

We have noted that General Florescu is considered the father of the Romanian army but he, in turn, looked upon the army as his family: *"A military unit is just like a family whose sons offer each other help, support, parental care and good example for the young."*[17]

In 1845, while he was an assistant of Prince Gheorghe Bibescu, Florescu published *Teoria darii la semn* (The Theory of the Target Shooting Practice) comprising a chart with images which explained the efficiency of the infantry rifle in terms of the number and speed of projectiles shot at a given target. *"Although the bayonets are largely used in wars, nowadays it is well known that the power of an infantry unit lies mostly in its rapid fire power."* The work was printed by Zaharia Carcalechi Publishing house, a well know publisher who encouraged the spread of military books. The book was also interesting because its transition alphabet was no longer dominated by Cyrillic characters.

The general also wrote a pamphlet entitled *"Exposition About the Improvement of the Romanian Army, 1859-61,"* published by the Stephan R. Rassidescu Press – a positive evaluation of his reforms under Cuza already alluded to.

Another work entitled "*Military Studies and Training*" dealt with the concern for the soldiers' food and health in time of peace and war. *"It is known, he stated, that most soldiers die because of decease rather than firepower."* He also emphasized the importance of the intendency and

[15]*Datoriile ostasului, a translation of General Florescu after the work of the French Captain Roqcancourt*, Bucharest, Socecu, Sander and Teclu, 1876, page 3 (in *Cours elementaire d'art et d'histoire militaire a l'usage des eleves de l'Ecole royale speciale militaire*, vol. I-IV. See Appendix.

[16]*Ibidem.* Pages 10-11; 13.

[17]*Ibidem,* page 25.

supply corps. Details about maneuvers were tackled for each arm: marches, cantonments, bivouacs calculated with respect to time and distance. General Florescu's defensive theories are ably summarized in a pamphlet entitled, "Fortifications" based on a speech he delivered to the Senate in 1899. While his stress on the importance of education for the army is well summarized in a pamphlet entitled, "The Institution of the Army Based on Schooling," published in 1855.[18]

To the end of his life Florescu remained receptive to everything new and his interests went well beyond military affairs. A telling comment by one of his friends sums up his optimism which characterizes the man: *"Doubt and skepticism, disillusionment or discouragement found no place in his heart. For him the word 'impossible' did not exist."*

Principally Florescu was a perpetual student and teacher, an exceptional instructor of the young generation of soldier-student. This last aspect represented perhaps the principal theme of his entire career as a military man and as a politician.

[18] *Institutiunea armata bazata pe scoala*, lecture delivered at the Romanian Athenaeum, February 14, 1888, Printing House of the Royal Court, Goble. Also see, *Osebirea intre armatele vechi si cele moderne*, Printing House of the Royal Court, Goble, 1890, and *Fortificatiunile*, a speech delivered in the Senate on May 7, 1889, published at the Printing House of the Royal Court, Goble.

CHAPTER VI

POLITICAL ACTIVITY DURING THE LAST DECADES OF HIS LIFE

For twelve years, during Ion Bratianu's governing, General Florescu had not involved himself in political life. But he came back to action when the so-called "united opposition" caused the downfall of the liberal government. Meanwhile he had become a member of the liberal-conservative movement which had been founded after several discussions based on an agreement which had been concluded between the Liberal Conservatives and Gheorghe Vernescu's liberal faction. According to this agreement, which General Florescu had also signed as head of the party, together with I. Bratianu, G. Vernescu, M. Kogalniceanu, A. I. Lahovari and General N. Haralambie, the members of the new political group promised not to engage in any coalition which could represent a personal advantage to any one of them.[1]

It was in this new capacity that General Florescu became President of the Senate, an important position since the Senate at that time had become a prestigious institution able to oppose and even impose its will upon an administration with which it disagreed. This was indeed the situation in the autumn of 1889 when the "Junimist" government composed of a coalition of liberal conservatives and pure conservatives wished to introduce certain policy changes in answer to a message from the throne (Romania had become a Kingdom in 1882). The majority of Senators did not accept the text proposed by the Council of Ministers and also opposed an amendment introduced by General Florescu who attempted to find a compromise solution in his capacity of President of the Senate. Bitter discussions followed in the Senate dividing the members into two factions, a fact which initially caused Florescu to resign. For a short interval the Presidency of the Senate was assumed by his old rival N. Kretulescu – but not for long. Florescu was soon re-elected to his former position as President of the Senate. In order to resolve the crisis King Carol finally nominated General Florescu to become Prime Minister for the second time on the 21st of February 1891 a position which he held until November of that year (the 22nd Ministry during his reign). This government was composed exclusively of Florescu's new liberal-conservative party members an honor which irritated Florescu's old ally and friend politician Lascar Catargiu, the head of the conservative party who had hoped to be

[1]Gheorghe Niculescu, *Parlamentul roman. Scurta expunere in ordine cronologica a regimului nostru parlamentar de la 1866 pana astazi*, Bucharest, 1903, page 502.

nominated himself, particularly on the year when the celebration of the King's 25 years of rule took place.[2]

During Florescu's premiership the moment had also arrived for the renewal of Romania's secret alliance (1883) with the Austro Hungarian Empire of which Germany and later Italy (in 1888) were members. It was initially signed for a five-year period and later to be renewed every three years automatically. The allies were to come to each others help in case of an unprovoked attack aimed at the Entente powers. The treaty kept in a secret vault in the royal palace at Sinaia was never submitted to Parliament and only known to the Bratianus and to Romania's representatives at Berlin. It is clear that, if known, Romanian public opinion which continued to be pro-French would have disapproved of it because of the oppression of the Romanian majority in Transylvania by the Hungarian authorities. In fact in 1890 an association called the League for the Cultural Unity of All Romanians was founded. Its first permanent secretary was Alexandru D. Florescu, my grandfather, and General Florescu's nephew. He also acted as the general's secretary and kept him regularly informed of Hungarian violations of the rights of the Romanian population in Transylvania. It is thus evident that General Florescu was also very much aware of the problem.

On September 18th King Carol left for Monza in Italy ostensibly to visit his wife Elizabeth of Wied, better known by her pseudonym as the writer "Carmen Sylva" who, following an illness, was recovering in the city of Palanza. However, in addition to visiting his wife the King had a far more delicate mission, namely that of consulting with King Victor Emanuel and the Italian Prime Minister di Rudini on whether it was in Romania's interest to renew the triple alliance for another three years given the delicate situation of Hungary's (Austria's partner in the dual monarchy) violation of the rights of the Romanian population of Transylvania which represented a majority of 3,000,000 inhabitants.[3] They both knew that the Italians themselves had their own problems with the Austrian authorities in the Italian Tyrol. To Florescu's surprise and consternation di Rudini spoke positively about the advantages of renewing the treaty on the road of completing the Italian Risorgimento. As a relative of the Kaiser, Austria's ally King Carol was acutely embarrassed by this difficult predicament. General Florescu however well informed of Hungary's violations took the lead in the discussion which followed. He curtly replied to di Rudini that Romania also intended someday to reunite all Romanians on both sides of the Carpathians. Only when that goal was achieved could truly friendly relations exist with the Austro Hungarian Empire. Clearly Florescu was

---

[2]Traian P. Lungu, *Viata politica in Romania la sfarsitul secolului at XIX-lea. 1888-1899*, Bucharest, 1967, page 98.

[3]"In a note written by Alexander Floresu (September 18, 1891) he stated: Romania has not fulfilled her secular dream of uniting under one king; General Florescu wishes it deeply."

opposed to renewal. It is likely that it was because of his views that Florescu lost his Prime Ministership. For on November 27th his old ally Lascar Catargiu was asked to form what has been termed "the great conservative coalition."[4] This may have been the meaning of the remark of historian Constantin Gane in his biography of Petre Carp to the effect that the King removed Florescu from his office of Premier "because of his lack of vision"[5] being opposed to the renewal of the secret Treaty with the Central Powers. Though Carol did all he could to persuade Emperor Francis Joseph to put pressure on the Parliament in Budapest, it is said that a room was permanently prepared for an imperial visit at the Palace in Sinaia. The Emperor never came and the King eventually renewed the secret alliance with Austria Hungary in 1892.

Nonetheless the King's personal friendship with Florescu continued. On December 1892 the General was invited to accompany the King Carol to Sigmaringen on the occasion of the wedding of Prince Ferdinand with Princess Marie, niece of Queen Victoria and Tsar Alexander II of Russia. Since Carol and Queen Elizabeth of Wied had only one daughter who died in infancy, the heir to the throne was Carol's nephew Prince Ferdinand of the Hohenzollern-Sigmaringen. Princess Marie noted in her memoirs that among the dignitaries in her entourage "Florescu was the only good looking one…who had a fine head and wore a pointed beard and huge mustache in the Second Empire style.[6]

From this point onwards the General stepped out of the political scene and remained in the shadow of a younger generation which replaced the elder political veterans. Among the new politicians who marched on to leading positions were figures such as another I. Bratianu, the son of the first Ion Bratianu, D. A. Sturdza on the liberal side, and Petre Carp and Tache Ionescu on the conservative side.[7]

Following his retirement Florescu took care of his properties at Vizuresti, Salcuti Odobesti, and certain cultural establishments such as the Romanian Athenaeum, whose members had elected him in 1865. He became one of the directors and often delivered lectures there. He was also re-elected President of the Society for the Education of the Romanian people.

His personal life was saddened by family problems. He did not get along with his second wife Alina Stirbey whom he had married in Dresden,

---

[4]Alexandru D. Florescu, the general's nephew and permanent secretary of the Cultural League met with King Carol I once a year in order to inform him on the situation of the oppressed Romanian citizens in Transylvania. See Radu A. Florescu, *Liga Culturala…*, December 2003.

[5]D. Costescu, *Fazele ministeriale in Romania…*, page 93.

[6]*Mary Queen of Romania, the Story of my Life*, page 282.

[7]Petre Carp, although pro-German was opposed to King Carol I even in 1870.

Germany. Eventually he had an affair with Iuliana Viisoreanu, (born Rosianu), but was not allowed to marry her. The child born out of wedlock was not immediately recognized by the family but in the end things were resolved.[8]

Towards the end of his life the General found time to take care of the peasants living on his estates who had great respect for him. He would build them decent homes, schools and churches, supply them with wood for heating their houses, and if the harvest failed he would supply them with money or corn. His greatest passion continued to be the village schools which he built, one at Salcuta, the other at Odobesti. Whenever he visited these villages he spoke to students and teachers, was interested in their welfare, paid for classroom materials, and rewarded the good teachers and students with end of year prizes and books.[9]

In Bucharest he spent a good deal of time as President of the Society for the Education of the Romanian people, and at the end of the year award ceremonies were held for talented students at the Romanian Athenaeum, which had opened when he became Prime Minister in 1891. During the last five years of his life he taught a course on military art at the Pedagogical Institute. In this connection it is relevant to quote from the memoirs of one of his veteran peasant soldiers, who eventually became a teacher in Gorj district.

"I have known the General since he was my teacher. We learned from him, among other things how to be patient in accomplishing goals. I shall never forget the General's deep tone of voice when he interrupted his lesson and gave us the following advice: 'do not expect, my boys, to find either happiness or easy living in the villages where you will teach. The honest and open-minded teacher will always come into conflict with the innkeeper, the leaseholder, the mayor and even the sub-prefect. You will often feel disgusted, tired, disappointed. You will encounter many obstacles and many annoyances on your way. Nevertheless my boys, do not lose your patience, let the bad days go away and think of the fact that teachers are helpful to your country. Think about me who struggled for 55 years and never felt despair.' Let's move ahead, God will always be with us[...]. Let's remember these words because we teachers have reasons to feel disappointed, tired and desperate during the school year."[10]

By the end of his life on October 12, 1889, General Florescu who was still passionate about uniforms and medals was honored by the French government with the distinction, "Grand Officer of the Legion of Honour." Still a close friend of the royal family, he would visit the King and Queen at

[8]His marriage to Alina Stirbey was very unhappy. Florescu was a spendthrift while his wife was avaricious. He also had an eye for beautiful women. His wife filed for divorce and accused him of adultery. The court granted him the divorce.

[9]Ionnescu-Gion, *Generalul Florescu*, pag 26.

[10]Citing one of Florescu's pupil's letter addressed to the audience by Eliza Michow.

the summer palace in Sinaia where members of the Florescu family took piano and violin lessons in the music room destined by Queen Carmen Sylva "for talented people," such as the composer George Enescu.[11]

When he became ill, in 1892, it was natural for him to return to France, the country where he had begun his military education. The poor condition of his health forced him to go to a sanatorium in Paris where he passed away on May 10, 1893, aged 74. In Paris he was honored by the President of France, Paul Cambon, as well as by other members of the French administration, by the Romanian Diplomatic Agent in Paris, Iancu Alecsandri, Vasile Alecsandri's brother, by representatives of the Romanian community and by the Second French Infantry Regiment in which he had served, as well as by Romanian officers from different French military schools who wanted to pay their final respects. According to his last wishes his body was brought back to his native country. The arrival of the funeral train in Bucharest on May 21 (old style calendar) occurred in an atmosphere of national mourning. The newspaper "Timpul" published a detailed description of the General's funeral: "On the platform of the North Stations there were family members, government representatives, active and reserve officers from the Capital's garrison, secretaries of the Ministry of War, a delegation of the conservative club, students of the 'Pedagogical School for the Education of the Romanian People,' the Patriarch's representative surrounded by the local clergy, etc. Carried by officers, soldiers and students, the coffin was set on a gun carriage, covered with a tricolor flag, on top of which were the sword and the cap of the deceased together with a garland made of laurel and oak leaves bearing the words 'General Florescu's army.' The carriage was pulled by eight black horses wearing a yellow harness led by gunner-conductors under a sergeant's command in formal dress. A military carriage bedecked with crowns of flowers followed. The funeral procession proceeded to the Serban Voda cemetery accompanied by the music of the military brass brand. The procession opened, followed by a squadron of gendarmes on horseback followed by members of the high clergy. The General's medals were carried on twelve velvet pillows by a major assisted by two captains. The General's horse bearing the ceremonial harness was led by a soldier behind the carriage. The carriage was held by the Prime Minister, Lascar Catargiu, Colonel Tell, G.

[11]General Florescu's first funeral took place on May 14 at the Romanian Church on the Saint Jean de Beauvais Street in Paris. The President of the French Republic, Paul Cambon, the Minister of War and the Minister of External Affairs, the High Chancellor of the Legion of Honor were represented there. The funerals were led by Emil Ghica, the General's son-in-law. Beside members of the Romanian delegation, there were also present Romanian officers who were studying in France, as well as important notabilities of the Romanian colony. Two infantry battalions, two squadrons of the naval artillery and a battery rendered military honors. After the funeral service the coffin followed by a numerous procession and by the legation's staff went to the East Station of Paris where it left for Bucharest.

Cantacuzino, chairman of the Senate, as well as by Generals Manu President of the Deputies' Assembly, Lahovari, Minister of War and Eraclie Arion, Commander of the Second Army Corps. The procession also included an empty royal carriage. A religious service was held at the new St. Gheorge Church. During the ceremony the guard of honor was comprised of soldiers and non-commissioned officers from all army branches as well as students of the 'Pedagogical School for the Education of the Romanian People. Prince Ferdinand, the Crown Prince also attended the ceremony accompanied by General Vladescu, head of the King's Military House, the lady of Honor, Mrs. Bengescu on behalf of Queen Elisabeth, and Mrs. Greceanu on behalf of the Crown Princess Mary."[12]

General Lahovary delivered a speech where he said among others: *"We have darkened our flags, our swords and our hearts because we have lost the leader who loved us most. Yes! He loved us with an endless love, he loved us and he educated us the leaders of his beloved army! He was never happier than when he was at the head of his troops! When he rode his horse with his medals on his chest accompanied by music he shouted, 'Bless you my children!' We all felt that his cry was happy and cheerful; we felt loved by him and our young hearts beat loud in our chests. At that moment we had the vision of a greater Romania! He was the first to teach us how to lead the troops in the complicated maneuvers of our small army at a time when the great armies of the world had not as yet begun such training."*

With the roar of artillery salvoes and the sound of bugles, the coffin was laid to rest by the officers, soldiers and students of the "Pedagogical School," whose teacher he had been all this time.

In the history of the Romanian army and the preparations for the War of Independence of 1877-1878, General Florescu fully deserved the title of "founder and organizer of the modern army" given by his friend, Vasile Alecsandri.

When he passed away some politicians who knew the General well and appreciated his contributions expressed the desire to erect a monument in his memory. A committee was thus formed by friends and members of his family, and a bust representing the General was cast in bronze and placed in front of the building of the Second Army Corps in Bucharest which later became the headquarters of the General Staff of the Romanian army. That bust was later placed in the Hall of the Romanian Athenaeum. Finally, on the occasion of the celebration of the centenary commemorating Romania's War of Independence, the statue was placed at the Central Military Museum in Bucharest where it is located to this day.

General Florescu's figure can also be seen on the pedestal of Prince Alexander Ion Cuza statue in the middle of Union Square in Iasi. The construction of this monument was ordered in 1903 but only completed in 1909 at the celebration of the passing of half a century since Cuza's Union

[12]See newspaper *Timpul*; in Appendix.

of the Principalities. The unveiling of this status was postponed because some politicians considered honoring Cuza inopportune and even dangerous to the Hohenzollern family in the years of international tension preceding World War I. However, wiser councils prevailed and eventually funds were raised by public subscription and a famous Italian sculptor was hired to complete the work. The unveiling took place in October 1912 in the presence of the King and members of the government. On the monument's pedestal, in addition to Florescu, were all the close advisors of the former Prince Cuza, Mihail Kogalniceanu, Costaehe Negri and Emanuel Kretulescu. Later this imposing monument was upgraded and a marble and granite base was fitted to the monument and placed in a proper environment: Union Square in the center of the city of Iasi in Moldavia.

CHAPTER VII

GENERAL FLORESCU – THE MAN AND HIS LEGACY

General Florescu, considered by many historians to be the father of the Romanian army, also was called by General Radu Rosetti "a forgotten man of history" in a commemorative conference which took place at the Romanian Academy in 1936. This forgetting of the military and political man may seem surprising at first and is hard to understand because there are hundreds of documents accessible concerning his life. His correspondence with the most important political and military figures of the time can be found in the various archives of the 1848 revolutionaries available at the Romanian Academy and, most of all, in Cuza's archive which was published under the care of the late professor Constantin Giurescu. Florescu's army reforms and his parliamentary speeches can be found in "Monitorul Oastei," which was founded by him, and in "Monitorul Oficial." The correspondence with King Carol I is included in the King's "Memoirs" and in the Hohenzollern Sigmaringen Archives in Germany.

A collection of personal letters is owed to the former Director of the Museum of the City of Bucharest, Gheorghe D. Florescu. The General's writings and speeches which were published in several treatises outline the fascinating contribution to Romanian military history of an officer who was also a pedagogue and a man of culture. Certainly there is enough material on Florescu to save him from being forgotten; although this "forgetting" can be explained. First of all, General Florescu worked in the shadow of great personalities, figures such as Prince Cuza, head of the army, an outstanding politician and Romanian patriot. But we must not forget that, although Cuza's name is always mentioned first whenever a reform was initiated by General Florescu, the Prince was not an experienced soldier. Although he had entered the army as a "Junker" from 1837 up to 1840 he was promoted officer only in 1857 by the Governor Nicolae Vogoride, with the rank of second lieutenant. There followed rapid promotions: lieutenant, captain, major, colonel and finally head of the Moldavian army in one year only! It is not surprising then that Prince Cuza approved almost all the army reforms initiated by Florescu who had a very significant military past. A second explanation would be that Florescu's most important reforms during 1871-1875 took place under King Carol's authority, a well-trained Prussian officer prestigious by virtue of his kinship with the new Emperor of Germany, after his victories against France. King Carol who knew Florescu's contribution to the organization of Cuza's army, approved almost all the reforms initiated under his authority, but the relationships between the two commanders had the nature of collaboration between two professionals.

An objective biographer cannot afford exaggerated praise such as those written on the occasion of Florescu's double funerals in May 1893 in Paris and then in Bucharest. But it is not proper either to be excessively impressed by the polemics directed against Florescu, written by his political opponents such as D. Sturdza and I. Bratianu. The tense atmosphere of public life in Bucharest in the second half of the 19th century encouraged the reader to sympathize with the poet Eminescu who calls Vlad the Impaler from his grave to impale "the crazy men and scoundrels" customary in political life. Praises for the General ceased almost completely during the era of the Bratianus liberal governments which dominate the Romanian political scene before and after the Great War. A rare exception was the contribution of the military historian, General Radu Rosetti writing during the inter-war period. During the communist regime it was understandable for historians not to mention General Florescu in their works because he belonged to an "unhealthy" social class.

The problem was partially resolved recently in the works of G. D. Florescu (former Director of the City Museum of Bucharest) who attempted to rehabilitate his ancestor's success. Florescu had all the qualities requisite for worldly success. He was good looking, charming and had the best education an aristocrat could afford at the time. If you look at his many portraits the viewer is impressed by his deep-set blue eyes which seem to watch you wherever you are. With his brown hair, oval face and regular features he certainly drew the attention of the fair sex. His pride, not to say arrogance--a weakness, was visible on his face. Many military men envied him for his medals and decorations which covered his chest starting with the French Legion of Honor. Cuza's private secretary, Baligot de Beyne, who generally admired the General, complained about the large number of letters sent to different heads of state under the title "Medals for General Florescu." Undoubtedly he was not only proud but also ambitious and no doubt his marriages helped his advancement. He got married twice and each time with the daughter of a Prince: the first time with Ecaterina, the daughter of Prince Gheorghe Bibescu and the second time with Alina, the daughter of Prince Barbu Stirbey. He was very vulnerable to the charms of the fair sex and probably unfaithful to Alina, a marriage which had been unhappy from the very start.

At an advanced age he indulged in a very personal correspondence with Pauline, Alecsandri's daughter. Later because of an accident he had difficulty in writing and used his daughter Catrina, the wife of Emanoil Ghica, as his secretary calling her "my little butterfly," a nickname coined by her father Alecsandri. At the end of his life he relied on his mistress Iuliana Visoianu, a woman who gave him an illegitimate child, later recognized by the family.

Chapter VII

In order to outline the positive aspects of his personality, Florescu was probably one of the most educated young boyars of the time. At first he studied at the famous National College of Saint Sava – the alma mater for all the future political leaders in Wallachia. Unlike Napoleon he excelled in most of the subjects under the guidance of the great Transylvanian teachers of the time. In 1836 he attended Louis le Grand Lyceum during four years and then spent another four years at the Army General Staff School, both in Paris. These studies represented a priceless instruction for a foreigner. The school director was General Jacques Aupick who had learned his military art from Napoleon himself. Florescu also met and admired Captain Rocquancourt another strategy and tactics specialist whose work, *A Soldier's Duties*, impressed him so much that he translated it into Romanian in 1844. He also reprinted it later in a textbook for the whole army. During the time spent in France he was promoted to the rank of lieutenant in the Second Infantry Regiment. After he had completed his patriotic education at St. Sava College, Florescu was deeply influenced during the nine years spent in France by the French military experience which provided him with qualifications which few Romanian boyars possessed at the time. Moreover this military experience ingratiated in him a feature which only a true soldier could understand completely: the sense of discipline and a strong loyalty towards the national colors which represented a soldier's oath of allegiance. These features almost destroyed his political career at the time. Florescu strongly believed in discipline and he remained a Conservative for the rest of his life although he never became a mere reactionary. He believed in the formula of Sir Robert Peel, head of the English Conservative Party, i.e., you must resist change as long as possible but only until change becomes unavoidable. Therefore reforms should be adopted slowly (the "peu à peu" philosophy). He was thus open to tergiversations and his political philosophy may be called "liberal-conservative."

His greatest weakness, the weakness of many military men, was that of times he was tempted to rely on force. This negative feature merged with his nationalist ideals and manifested itself in a lack of tolerance for ethnic minorities and specifically the Jews. He was convinced that a soldier must be a native and should not have the right to vote.

Given all these advantages Florescu could hardly fail to make his way in life but his ascension was truly meteoric. He also owed much to his marriages. Lieutenant at age 22 in 1842 the following year he became a special assistant of Prince Bibescu and captain at age 24.

Two years later his wedding present was the promotion to the rank of major. On the eve of the 1848 Revolution, at age 29, he was advanced to the rank of colonel and then, in 1860, Cuza appointed him a general. Besides his military career he occupied other positions, for instance, Governor of Prisons. His enemies claimed that his elegant house in Bucharest was built by prisoners who had been sent from the salt mines precisely for this purpose. He was also a member in the Commission in charge of the foundation of an officers' school. In his spare time he started writing books on tactics and strategy. From the historians' point of view, the first stage in Florescu's career, during the Reglement period imposed by the Russians, is less interesting. His only undisputable achievement at that time was the foundation of a Romanian artillery unit with several cannons offered by the sultan as a gift in 1842.

The 1848 Revolution caught young Florescu by surprise and isolated him from other family members who had jointed the revolutionary forces. He kept his promise as a soldier loyal to his oath, and remained by Bibescu's side the moment when a first shot ripped off the Prince's epaulette. Nevertheless, this episode created an embarrassing situation for Florescu because when he was a student in Paris he sympathized with certain goals of the conservative forty-eighters. However, when the army refused to protect the Prince against the revolution, Florescu requested that the guilty officers be punished. Once the provisional government took over, he was one of the few Wallachians who fought with the Russian troops in Transylvania against the Hungarian revolutionaries. He was attached to General Lüders who collaborated with Avram Iancu and his cohorts of Mountaineers from the Apuseni region.

His role in Russian ranks against the Hungarians was rewarded by Tsar Nicolas II with one of the medals which adorned his chest. After the dissolution of the revolutionary government, Florescu regained almost all the offices he had occupied during Bibescu's rule. He also came to the helm of the Ministry of Education, Public Works and Communications. At the same time he was the first teacher of tactics and strategy at the new military school. The brief Austro-Russian occupation during the Crimean War led him to embark on the most controversial action in his entire career. Because he was a very close friend of General Lüders, he was one of the three Romanian boyars who fought with the Russians in the Crimea. Service in the Russian armies represented in fact the most useful war experience of his entire career. But as a result of the victory of the French-English allies his pro-Russian activity, which was severely criticized by the English consul Colquhoun, made his resignation from the army unavoidable.

As a nationalist, Florescu always believed that the Union of the Principalities was imminent. A contemporary foreign source suggested that he could have been an acceptable candidate for the throne of the United Principalities. Florescu's enemies accused him of having had exaggerated ambitions at the time and even later, when they blamed him for certain intrigues to obtain the throne of Bulgaria. These assertions were not founded. In 1859 Florescu did not abandon his old loyalties and we find him actively promoting Bibescu's candidacy against the radicals who supported Golescu. It is undeniable that the political maneuvers of the conservative forces took place in his own house in Bucharest. When he realized that there were not enough votes to support Bibescu's candidacy, Florescu played a crucial part in convincing the entire party to vote for Alexandru Ioan Cuza. It is very significant that shortly after Cuza's election, Bratianu embraced him on both cheeks. In return, Cuza rewarded him with the office of Ministry of War and offered him an historical friendship for life.

Florescu started his military career during the regime of the Organic Statutes sponsored by Russia under Princes Bibescu and Stirbey, as head of a small police force which was striving to liberate itself from Russian influence. Cuza's coming to the throne of the United Principalities in 1859, actually the entire Cuza epoch until the very eve of his abdication in 1866, reveal a crucial period in the General's career when he laid the foundations of the future Romanian army. Later, during King Carol's rule and with his help, Florescu succeeded in improving upon the more humble army framework he had built during Cuza's rule and began organizing and training an army able to launch an offensive beyond Romania's borders which he knew was essential to secure the country's independence.

As a politician and a teacher, Florescu occupied many positions in various governments as Minister of Internal Affairs, Public Works, Communications and Cults. He was elected Deputy, Senator and later President of the Senate. In 1876 and 1891 he became Prime Minister twice. He was not very successful in his career as a Parliamentarian because he was not a convincing public speaker. He showed special concern for road building essential for transporting goods and troops between Bucharest and Iasi; he also made efforts to beautify Bucharest and drew attention to the floods caused by the overflow of the Dambovita River in the Capital. He also insisted on organizing Cismigiu Park, a famous landmark in the Capital. The costs for all these goals were contested by his political opponents.

In his view being an educator was a profession almost as important as his military career. He was fond of the title of "teacher" and took pleasure lecturing for over 25 years at the War Academy and later at the Romanian Athenaeum. By the end of his life he held different courses in elementary schools which he founded near his country estates. He also enjoyed lecturing on military affairs comparing famous battles of ancient civilizations with those of modern times, though much of his focus centered on Romania's struggle for survival.

Florescu was accused on being pro-Russian, pro-French and even pro-German. As he had served all the three powers, it is obvious that during his long career these countries noticed such orientations though in the end most of his loyalties belonged to France, which represented his important second fatherland. We might compare Florescu's answers to such so-called "tergiversations" by paraphrasing Lord Palmerston, a great English statesman of the period: *"Romania has neither eternal friends nor eternal enemies; only the interests of the country are everlasting."*

General Florescu was faithful to the Romanian Orthodox Church and he understood the importance of religion for the army's spiritual needs. Therefore, he appointed priests to serve in every regiment. According to his nationalist principles, he favored the autocephaly of the Romanian Orthodox Church which undermined and offended the authority of the Constantinople Patriarchy and sometimes even the King.

In order to make a final evaluation of General Florescu's military career the historian must be objective and take into account the positive elements as well as the imperfections of his policy and personality. When discussing great military commanders such as a Napoleon or a von Moltke who were brilliant masters in the art of strategy and tactics, and developed new concepts of war, it was obvious that with his modest experience Florescu did not fit among this category of men. We may add that he never had the chance to wage a major war. However, considering his emphasis on fortifications, I suppose he might have been an acceptable "defensive general." Rather than a field commander, perhaps he more aptly played the part of a war theoretician, a military pedagogue for next to the "great captains of history." There is still room for the less fascinating but equally important "organizers of victory" such as Lazare Carnot who planned the victories of the French revolutionary armies without whom Napoleon would not have gained his remarkable victories.

In the writing of this book, I do not intend to present Florescu as a great man who represented an idea, like Cuza or Balcescu. Nevertheless, his achievement in organizing the modern Romanian army was a very important step which had a decisive influence on the victories attained on the battlefield in 1877-78.

He was a good historian and perhaps a prophet of the military and political future. There is no doubt he would have been proud of the day the author of this monograph had the privilege of witnessing, at the White House in Washington, D.C., the tricolor flag of Romania drawn by Cuza and Florescu waving in the sunset during the historic moment when Romania entered NATO. This was an important stage in the evolution of Romania's modern army which Florescu founded and nurtured.

APPENDIX

I. E. FLORESCU'S LETTER ADDRESSED TO G. H. BIBESCU

January 8/20, 1857. I. E. Florescu's letter addressed to G. H. Bibescu, the Prince of Wallachia who was in Constantinople. It concerned the political situation in Bucharest, the elections for the ad-hoc assemblies and the arrival of the representatives of the seven powers in accordance with the stipulations of the Paris Agreement.

In the original document written by Florescu in French on the frontispiece is the reproduction of a stamp with an imaginary view of Bucharest (Inventory no. 25028). The lithograph was made at Lith.anst.v.Wilh.Breicha in Bucharest.

The Bucharest History Museum
Inventory No. 25028, No. S.C. 6011/57, No. 22

Monseigneur,

Depuis la derniere letter que j'ai eu l'honneur d'adresser a Votre Altesse a Constantinople, j'ai pu enregistrer les faits suivants qui dans les circonstances troubles, meritent quelque attention. Le Caïmacam vient de s'installer a l'ancien Palais, comme pour mieux faire sentir la solidite de sa position a l'occasion du jour de l'an, avec les mutations et les nominations qu'il a faites dans l'ordre judiciaire. Il a accorde en meme temps, a titre de gratification, les appointements pour trois mois aux officiers de tout grade ainsi qu'a d'autres personnes dont les unes ne comptent pas meme parmi les fonctionnaires publics. Le tout montant au chiffre d'environ 600000 piastres. On dit que le Caïmacam va continuer ce systeme de largesses et que bientot il doit accorder a tous les fonctionnaires civiles, trois mois d'appointements, au dessus (sic) de cinq cent piastres. Ces traits de generosite ou plutot de prodigalite dans un moment ou il declare lui-meme les finances, dans un etat absolu de detresse ont ceci d'alarmant qu'ils prouvent jusqu'a l'evidence, l'intention dans laquelle ils sont faits. C'est triste que contrairement a l'esprit meme du traite de Paris, on ait donne a un gouvernement provisoire de tels moyens de seduction, sans parler de la liste civile qui est encore un levier puissant entre les mains d'un homme qui ne vise qu'a se menager un parti pour sortir victorieux de la lutte qui se prepare. Pour ma part, je ne crois pas un seul instant au success d'un homme qui etait deja connu et qui s'est porte un dernier coup, par ses propres actes, pendant les quelques mois de sa Caïmacamie. Mais en meme temps, on ne comprend pas comment les homes d'etat qui s'occupent de notre future organization, ne sentent pas l'inconvenient, l'injustice, le scandale meme, d'un tel etat de choses. Aussi, tous les hommes serieux pensent chez nous que les pouvoirs de la Caimacamie devraient cesser, ou du moins, etre considerablement limites, a l'epóque de l'arrivee des Commissaires a Bucarest. Sans quoi, a en juger par ce qui arrive dans les pays meme les plus eclaire de l'Europe, on doit s'attendre a ce que tout soit fausse chez nous, jusqu'aux Elections (sic). Tous ces Messieurs, que je n'ai pas besoin de nommer ici, m'engagent d'ecrire a Votre Altesse pour lui signaler ce danger, afin qu'Elle tache par tous les moyens, de fixer l'attention de qui de droit sur une question aussi importante.

Un des derniers traits du Caimacam qui n'est certes pas fait pour combler le vide qui se fait chaque jour dans les rangs de son parti, est le suivant: Il vient de nommer a la censure au Secretariat d'Etat, un certain *Caliarhi* tout a fait etranger au pays. C'est un jeune homme de Constantinople qui accompagnait Kiamil-bey, porteur du firman d'installation de la Caimacamie. Cette nominatin qui nous rameme au temps des phanariotes, a provoque dans tous les parties une veritable indignation.

Relativement a Votre Altesse, je dirai sans crainte de m'abuser, que l'opinion lui est de plus en plus favorable. On dirait que les traits que lui lancent certains individus se retournent contre eux-memes, ainsi depuis quelques jours, on repand le bruit que Votre Altesse n'aurait eu aucune mission a Constantinople et qu'Elle y aurait ete meme mal reçu, que les autorites Turques (sic) se seraient formalisees de ce qu'Elle aurait visite en premier lieu les representants des Puissances etrangeres. Mais comme je viens de le dire, les sympathies augmentent pour Votre Altesse en raison des insinuations malveillantes que l'on se plait a repandre sur son compte.

Je m'empresse, Monseigneur, de vous faire parvenir une nouvelle publication qui vient de paratre. Elle est de Bozianu. Celui-ci se conduit depuis quelque temps en veritable parvenu. Il est de tous les parties etant surtout de celui de Demettre Ghika, dans l'espoir d'etre un jour son premier Ministre. C'est du reste un homme qui ne jouit d'aucune influence et je suis fache de l'avoir represente un jour a votre Altesse d'une maniere plus flatteuse qu'il ne le meritait.

Plusieurs jeunes gens, que j'evitais plutot que je ne frequentais; de ces jeunes gens qui se croient seuls patriotes et qui on fait dernierement encore le malheur du pays, sont venues a moi pour me parler de votre Altesse de la maniere la plus avantageuse. Malgre la defiance qu'ils pouvaient m'inspirer, j'ai ete loin de les repousser et grace a certains conseils que j'ai puise dans votre derniere lettre, j'ai pu a peu pres leur tenir langage : Nous nous trouvons a une epoque ou tout homme qui aime son pays doit faire abstraction des personnes, comme aussi, doit eviter de toucher aux questions de detail. Ces questions etant les seules sur lesquelles il nous etait permis de differer d'opinion, que pour le moment nous devions nous occuper que des bases fondamentales de l'organisaton du pays et qu'a cet egard Votre altesse avait bien voulu me poser quelques principes que j'ai pense pouvoir leur communiquer. Ils admirent l'esprit patriotique et desinteresse qui les ont dictes et declarerent que ce programme serait le leur, comme aussi, que nous devions nous entendre pour le faire comprendre et adopter par le plus de personnes que possible. Cet incident me donna l'idee et Monsieur Barbu Catargi est de cet avis, de faire publier le dit programme precede d'un petit preambule renfermant des conseils a nos compatriotes sur la ligne de conduite que chacun devrait tenir au moment ou le travail de reorganisation viendrait a commencer. J'expose ce fait a Votre Altesse, afin (sic) que si le temps le lui permet et qu'elle le juge convenable, elle veuille bien m'eclairer a cet egard par quelques nouveaux conseils.

Pour ce qui est de la maison, je viens prier Votre Altesse de vouloir bien m'autoriser d'une maniere precise a lui en arreter une, car toute maison (sic) qui serait encore disponible a Bucarest, ne saurait lui convenir a moins de temps et de travaux considerables. Une combinaison qui me parait plus heureuse est celle de menager a Votre Altesse, simplement un pied a terre, en atendant que nous puissions rafraichir l'ancien palais de la Metropole. Dans le cas ou Votre Altesse adoptait cette combinaison, Elle devrait faire en sorte que le Pacha reçut l'ordre d'evacuer le dit palais aussi vite que possible. De cette maniere nous aurions encore assez de temps pour y faire des travaux d'assainissements par Votre Altese.

Catherine a remis une lettre pour Votre Altesse au prince Georges Stirbey qui est parti ce matin pour Constantinople. Je remets la mienne a Monsieur Beclard qui veut bien se charger de vous la faire parvenir par l'entremise de l'Ambassade de France.

J'ai l'honneur d'etre, Monseigneur, avec le plus profond respect, de Votre Altesse le tres devoue.

I.E.
FLORESCO

P.S. J'oubliais, Monseigneur, une question des plus importantes: celle de la composition du Divan qu'on a deja dit resolue d'une maniere regrettable, car le bruit etait que la 1 ere Classe des Boyards, c'est a dire celle qui est composee, a peu d'exceptions pres, des personnes rompues aux affaires, connaissant mieux l'Etat du pays et ne partageant pas les idees subversives qui malheureusement infestent depuis quelque temps notre jeunesse et qui paraissent gagner le petit proprietaire et surtout notre clerge, les plus ignorants etant naturellement aussi les plus dangereux. On dit que la lere classe ne sera pas representee directement, mais qu'elle sera comprise dans la masse des proprietaires, qui devrait fournir deux deputes par district.

Dans ce cas, j'affirme, et c'est l'avis des personnes les plus sensees, qu'aucun homme de poids n'arrivera au Divan, car il a contre eux non seulement l'antipathie des petits proprietaires, mais encore, que ces derniers forment la grande majorite. C'est pourquoi je viens au nom des personnes animees des meilleurs sentiments, prier Votre Altesse, s'il en est temps encore, d'intervenir que le lere Classe soit representee par un nombre de deputes, dont le minimum devrait etre 17, celui des districts. Sans quoi, il est plus sure que le Divan qui va decider de l'avenir du pays, sera compose de simples paysans, de quelques petits proprietaires, suffisants et par cela memes ignorants, et quelques pretres aussi ignorants que malveillants.

Appendix

ORDER HANDED BY COLONEL I.E. FLORESCU TO PRINCE ALEXANDRU IOAN CUZA ON APRIL 9, 1860, CONCERNING STATIONING TROOPS IN BUCHAREST

9 avril 1860

J'ai toujours pensé que le devoir de tout Ministre de Guerre etait celui de prendre des dispositions telles qu'il puisse faire face a une eventualite quelconque. A part l'incurie de la plus part de mes prédécesseurs, je dois avouer que celui-la meme qui aurait au plus haut degre le sentiment de l'honneur mais qui negligerait de prendre a temps des mesures precises et énergique s'exposerait a la honte de se voir reduit a l'impuissance au moment voulu et paralyserait du meme coup ceux qui se trouveraient sous ses ordres.

Telles sont les considerations que j'il l'honneur de presenter a Votre Altesse.

Des que les moindres rumeurs se feraient sentir en ville, les troupes stationnees en garnison dans les casernes de Malmaison et Dealul Spirei, se mettraient en marche et par les plus courtes distances designees d'avance, prendront position.

1. A la Métropole — Le bataillon d'artillerie
Le bataillon a cheval (la batterie)
Un escadron de lanciers

2. Place du théâtre — Un détachement de gendarmes
Deux compagnies d'infanterie

3. Chemin de Ramnic — Deux compagnies d'infanterie
La batterie a pied
Un escadron de lanciers

4. A la Police — Les Pompiers
Un détachement de gendarmes

L'efficacité de ces detachements varient en raison de la force des troupes de garnison. Il resulte de cette disposition que la Metropole, la police, la place du theatre et celle de Ramnic sont quatre points fortement occupes dont les trois derniers forment le triangle strategique, determine sur la carte ci-jointe et dont l'un des cotes passent par la cour du palais. Disseminer davantage les troupes ferait une faute tandis que d'apres ces disposition on les aurait sous main et selon le cas qui pourrait se presenter sur tel point et dans tel quartier de la ville on formerait des colonnes auxquelles on donnerait des missions speciales.

Pour tout ce qui regarde le detail d'execution les ordres sont faits en triples exemplaires sous la signature du Ministre de la guerre dont l'un devrait etre confie au chef de la police, le second au commandant de la place et le troisieme chez le ministre.

Ce qui precede suppose une confiance et une entente parfaite entre ces trois personnes. Aujourd'hui, la situation est changee par la nomination d'un prefet etranger aux convenances militaires. C'est donc le ministre et le commandant qui doivent seuls disposer de la force armee, des lors des troupes tels que les pompiers qui se sont trouves jusqu' a ce jour sons l'autorite de la police doivent immediatement et exclusivement passer sous celles du commandant militaire. Votre Altesse comprendra la responsabilite qui pese sur moi et sur le Colonel Cretzulesco et ne voudra pas permettre que notre autorite fut affaiblie ce qui rendrait nos responsabilites illusoires. Aussi apres une entente entre nous deux, nous prenons la resolution de vous soumettre, Monseigneur, le projet ci-joint d'ordonnance en attendant que Votre Altesse designe un commandant de troupes conformement a son ordre du jour du 7 janvier de cette annee. Cette mesure ne saurait blesser en rien le nouveau chef de la police car elle est pratiquee dans tous les pays ou le chef de la police n'est point militaire.

Le lieutenant Falcoyanu de l'Etat Major General que j'ai charge de ma presente depeche pourra donner a Votre Altesse des explications sur le fait tres regrettable et qui prouve encore une fois le degre de demoralisaton ou sont arrives jusqu'uns de nos officiers. C'est le lieutenant Cretzianu qui en pleine ceremonie a la Metropole, la nuit de Paques, ayant ete invite par le commandant a venir prendre le souper chez moi, a juger a propos de lancer des jurons apres quoi et au scandale du corps d'officiers et du public s'est refuse d'aller aux arrets non sans raisonner et vociferer. Par un de mes rapports, je soumets a Votre Altesse sa mise en jugement.

Je saisis cette occasion pour prier Votre Altesse de vouloir bien nous mettre Catherine et moi au pied de la Princesse. (The Romanian Academy, letter S26 (I-40)).

A SOLDIERS DUTIES*

My comrades-in-arms,

The gratitude that I feel toward Captain J. Rocquancourt for his useful lessons and at the same time I wish to see this kind of writing become familiar to us. I am also impelled to disclose a small segment of army history which deals with the soldier's duties, his needs, discipline and the genuine army spirit. I consider myself fortunate to translate in our language and to share with you this work which outlines the principles that make an army function, principles which are explained by a first rate author. Please read them with good-will because the author offers them with an open heart.

Sincerely,
Your Comrade-in-arms,
Captain I.E. Florescu

BRIEF OVERVIEW OF A SOLDIER'S DUTY

It is not enough to gather recruits and to disperse them in the different branches of an army. They must also learn how to use a rifle and be acquainted with the regulations which establish its specific movements. In this manner every soldier will be fully aware of the precision of his duty.

The soldier must discharge the order which are given to him, the more he departs from regulations, the weaker his position becomes.

Marching is one of the most important parts of the army's education because the more or less difficult the movement of any army results in more or less decisive events.

People from antiquity who did not have permanent armies would sometimes call to arms all the citizens who were able to fight and they would train them for wars using different methods. Veges [Vegetius] states that when the Roman Republic was flourishing the recruits would practice every day, in the morning and in the evening so that they get used to handling the weapons. Even the older soldiers would gather on the field of Mars where they performed different kinds of army exercises.

Their goal was war. They thought about it all the time. The sight of gladiators was very appreciated by the Romans precisely because it represented the livelier image of a war.

When the armies became permanent, they stopped calling citizens to arms except in cases when a great danger imposed such measures. The rest of the time legions would be called to arms with only a portion of the citizens and only for a limited period of time.

A soldier's knowledge must always fit the needs he might have during a day on the battlefield. His moves must be quick, simple and well coordinated: in tactics anything in excess may be harmful, because when a soldier's memory is burdened with unnecessary details he might even forget the things which are really important to him.

The writer Guibert states :

'A soldier's education should include three major points : 1. Physical training ; 2. Handling weapons and watching the progress made ; 3. Imagining different situations which may occur in war. It would be useless to speak of the significant aspect of a soldier's education which concerns courage and habits which inspire noble feelings. This aspect which is very useful has been neglected up to now and if we look for it in history we would find only one person who said, It's not enough for my soldiers to be brave, I also want them to be honest people.'

You must not think that Guibert's observation is shallow and unfounded. Who can deny today that discipline is based on tolerant behavior. It could never weaken a soldier's energy and courage. An aggressive soldier can never defeat a gentle but disciplined soldier. According to Branton the plunderers never have a chance to win a battle.

Unlike a soldier, an officer should not limit his knowledge to understanding mechanical movements; knowledge is based on a great deal of information which he must study thoroughly in theory if he wants to get good results in practice.

It would be undoubtedly wrong to ask a platoon commander to do something that only a general can do. Nevertheless an officer must be well prepared so that when he advances to a higher rank he should be able to discharge his new duties. An officer must always be ready to discharge the responsibilities corresponding to two or three higher ranks and not only in his branch of service but also in all other branches.

The peoples of Antiquity were very concerned with teaching and forming young men who later were given certain orders. That happened at a time when scientific knowledge was not as advanced and therefore the commanders' duties were much more limited. They performed fewer maneuvers where the officers could distinguish themselves through their knowledge and their skills. Such as the choice of the correct position, so important today, was completely neglected by them; they could only fight on open fields because of their weapons. On the contrary we often avoid plains and look for places which, by their physical location, allow us to use our power more effectively. The artillery and the fortifications, assault and defense are reasons why military operations today are very difficult and require a very thorough knowledge.

Science is close to warfare and the use of weapons has reached such an improvement and precision that a military education requires today the most attentive concern. A soldier must have knowledge of maps, topography, statistics, artillery, fortifications, assault and defense of cities, military administration and legislation, tactics and strategy. Apart from this knowledge the soldier must study history, geography and notions of physics and mathematics. All this knoweldge represents an introductory knowledge which cannot be acquired in school but only through an elaborate study of the most significant wars. Nobody should ever think that we ask too much of our officers, because otherwise how could they ever be entrusted with the lives of our citizens, the glory and the destiny of their country ? *The young man who is not able to discharge the hard and sacred duty of an officer should be promoted with difficulty.* Those who today consider this as a means of spending one's youth on leisure should better follow another career and make room for the person who is aware of his responsibilities; *in the army any reward is dangerous if it is not offered according to merit.*

The soldier of any rank must never forget that he owes obedience and respect to his superiors; he must be just, determined and at the same time tolerant towards the soldiers who are of lower rank; he also must discharge his duties with the greatest zeal and with the purest heart: he must be the friend of those who are his equals. He must be aware that everybody is watching and judging him: his most insignificant action will be remembered by his commanders, and his comrades-in-arms.

The spirit which inspires a soldier represents the real power of the state and not their number; here by spirit we understand the enthusiasn which, according to one of the authors of our century, enable us to dedicate our life to pain, death, and all kinds of privations, fatigue and discontents and finally that enthusiasn which makes us forge ourselves for the glory of our country. The genuine military spirit is found among all the conquering nations.

In ancient times the word discipline had a broader meaning than it has today. First of all discipline teaches everyone to obey the orders of the leader who watches and takes care of everybody's needs. It also turns into the instinct of the recruit to join the rows of soldiers in order to add his power to the power of his comrades-in-arms. A veteran soldier knows it through experience and practice.

Discipline also teaches respect for customs, for the property and for the population where the war takes place. This is a very significant point; the army which understands this meaning of discipline deserves our entire consideration. Unfortunately war does not accept this kind of discipline. If Napoleon had respected it entirely he would not have accomplished his goals. The man who aimed at the conquest of Europe could not obey a regular war system. His system which nobody should use thoughtlessly served his goal; nevertheless he failed because there are limits which cannot be crossed without endangering human powers. In the civilized nations there is no better way to preserve discipline than through religion. The worst enemies of discipline are: bad habits, laziness and punishment which generates insubordination and revolt.

A military unit is just like a family in which the sons must offer each other help, support; the oldest must secure parental care and good example for the youngest. If he wants to be honored by others a soldier must be aware of his own honesty: bad habits such as laziness, ignorance of religious principles, dissoluteness, cowardice, immoderate harshness toward the humble, represent many dangers that a soldier should avoid. A man who has become prey to these vices ceases to be a part of it because his comrades-in-arms would be the first to abandom him. Their voices would be heard by the authority whose most sacred mission is not to allow someone's dishonesty to cause any damage to the entire unit. A vicious soldier could only cause trouble in his social relationships; he would never be a good comrade and at the same time the nation could never rely on him in critical times.

The End (Translation from French made by I.E. Florescu; Bucharest, the Printing House of St. Sava College, 1844).

THE LETTER ADDRESSED BY GENERAL FLORESCU TO HIS FRIEND VASILE ALECSANDRI

Bucharest, February 8/20, 1878

Dear Alecsandri,

The letter which you sent me is my only great satisfaction after all the deceptions which I have lived lately. It will remain a valuable document for my children and a dear memory of the things I did for the progress of our army.

To the best interest of the Institution which is still functioning in our poor country, you come and pay homage to the faithfulness I swore. You must be certain, my dear Alecsandri, that the words which you spoke will find an echo in the hearts of our officers. They will find a way of resisting culpable intrigues which are woven around them by the persons who knew how to stigmatize so well with ugly words.

You have probably already found out from the latest newspapers about how Maiorescu's election was postponed to the Greek calendar indefinitely. We shall see what will happen to my election; the so-called Liberals are at ease because they are no longer under any control and even on the verge of disaster; M.S. will continue to shout: ' I am constitutional!'

You already know, my dear Alecsandri, the way the ministers withdrew their accusations. This action was as infamous as the accusation itself. But why should I go on talking to you about such a disgrace when we are on the verge of losing Bessarabia or better yet we have already lost it at Livadia!

I feel the need to see you; tell me what you are planning to do and when can I find you at Mircesti. I would gladly come there to spend some time together for a couple of days.

My whole family sends you their best regards. After I read the letter which you had sent me something happened which impressed me very much. A friend of mine thought he could take it with him in order to copy it, but Alina and my daughters suddently dashed at him and took the letter from his hands. They were urged by the same desire to keep a document so dear to my family! I was deeply touched by this scene and I told myself with tears in my eyes: where is Alecsandri to see them!...

Where are the young Catardjis? Wherever they are my children ask you to tell them how is Madame Catardji because they have hearsd she was not very well.

I end my letter by expressing my sadness when I heard through your lyrics of Rola's death, who, as you state it so well, went to join Cuza and Negri. I often wonder what these people would say if they came back to life. I think they would rather return to their tombs if they saw the results of envy and hatred.

Your old and sincere friend,
Florescu

P.S. The infirmity of my right hand forces me to use the help of a secretary. Nevertheless you will forgive me for that when I tell you that my secretary is someone you used to call once, ‘My Little Butterfly.’

AN EPISODE FROM THE LIFE OF I.E.M. FLORESCU

General I.Em. Florescu's mortal remains were brought to Bucharest yesterday and they will be entombed in the grave with proper honors.

Every country has its own people to be proud of.

Romania was proud of General Florescu as the man who was almost entirely the organizer of the Romanian army.

He honored his country during his lifetime and after his death. We must not forget that the French army presented military honors and saluted the mortal remains of General Florescu who passed away in Paris.

The Romanian government, faithful of the nation's feeling, will set up an even more imposing ceremony which, according to the program, will take the form of a posthumous tribute of respect paid by the Romanian army to its father.

I can still see that majestic, grandiose, imposing and sympathetic figure.

I had the chance to know him in person. He was delicate, affable, noble, loyal and fair-minded: a true gentleman. I therefore knew him well; but I do not want to write a biography nor his panegyric. My heart is still bewailiing the loss of this patriotic man with conservative-liberal and democratic inclinations. That was the reason why I was and I remained one of his most devoted friends.

Sometime and somewhere else if God will allow me I shall try to write the biography of the unforgettable General Florescu as a military man, as a politician, as a person who encouraged the spread of education. In this respect we must remember that General Florescu, returning from abroad, became a teacher at the military school, a trustee of the public schools and when he grew older became president of the 'Society for the Education of the Romanian People.' Besides the important donations made to this society, he would go there every morning in order to teach the students. We must not forget that during that time he was a member and supporter of the Romanian Athenaeum.

Nevertheless seeing that the Romanian army pays its posthumous respect to the mortal remains of General Florescu at the funeral ceremony I cannot help thinking of an episode from his military life.

It was around 1877-1878 when Romania was forced by circumstance to enter the war between Russian and Turkey.

The Romanian army aligned on the Danube line was ready to fight on the Bulgarian fields.

The army was ready to go to war and as Theodor Vacarescu stated: 'the soldiers' looking with pride and determination were ready to sacrifice their lives cheerfully on an order, a word, even a sign from their superior officers. General Florescu also asked to participate in the battle but nobody listened to him! He who had dedicated his entire life to the organization of the Romanian army in order to bring it closer to our ancestors' glory, he who was the organizer [...] and the father of the army, he was dismissed!

There is neither the time nor the place to judge the envy and the hatred which caused his removal.

All I can say is that this cruel removal caused grief to his heart and I shall never forget the day when I saw tears in the eyes of this old soldier, of this man inured to political fights, of this man who had faced so many disappointments in his life without complaining!

His heart was overwhelmed by sorrow because of this unfortunate removal!

The sense of justice seemed to stir up indignation and suddenly the powerful voice of the immortal V. Alecsandri, the poet who had praised the courage of the Romanian army in the last war echoed the feeling of the entire nation, in a letter addressed to General Florescu and published at the time:

'On the remote fields of death we looked in despair
To seek for the light of your old spear
The whole army increased the power of its fire
And asked to hear your voice in the cannnons' roar.
Because you made this army so lively, brave and young
Under the rules of Cuza and that of King Carol,
You should have had the honor to lead us in the battle
As you are the organizer, the man who made it happen.

My friend, be at rest and comfort your grief...
In every soldier today find your relief,
Because every Romanian knows and feels inside
That the ancestors' sword received with you more light.
And when you watch the flag with your eyes amazed
The living colors quiver in a majestic wave.'

Today the flag is waving on the cold chest of General Florescu and unfortunately you cannot warm it and bring him back to life so that he could see that the Romanian army has not forgotten her father!

G. Marian ('Timpul,' Sunday, May 23/June 4, 1893)

BIBLIOGRAPHY

PUBLISHED RESOURCES

- *Acte si documente relative la istoria Renasterii Romaniei*, vol. I, Bucharest, 1888.
- *Anuarul Armatei Românei I*, Bucharest, 1870-1920, the Ministry of War after 1883.
- *Armata romana*, National Printing House, Bucharest, contractor C.M. Radulescu.
- *Armata romana in timpul ultimilor 40 ani 1866-1906*. The central administration of the war. First part. The Ministry of War during the last 40 years, Bucharest, 1906.
- *Colectia vechilor legiuiri administrative, Regulamentele organice ale Valahiei si Moldovei*, Bucharest, 1944.
- *Documente privind istoria Romaniei. Rascoala din 1821. Documente interne*, vol. II, Bucharest, Academy Publishing House, 1959.
- *Reformele romanilor sau colectiune de toate legile si regulamentele introduse in administratia Romaniei de la 1858 January pâna la 1864 October*, Bucharest, 1864.

PERIODICALS

- "Albina romaneasca," 1830.
- "Academia romana. Memoriile sectiunii istorice."
- "Buletinul Muzeului Militar National," 1937-1942.
- "Monitorul Oastei" 1859-1882.
- "Monitorul Oficial" 1877-1879.
- "Revue Roumaine d'Histoire" (R.R.H.).
- "Revue historique du Sud – Est Europeen"
- "Studii si materiale de muzeografie si istorie militara," Central Military Museum.
- Magazin istoric

Bibliography

GENERAL WORKS

- Algiu Ioan (general), *Legi si ordonante militare*, vol. I-II, Bucharest, printing House of the Ministry of War, 1865.
- Angelescu, Constantin C., *Dezvoltarea constitutionala a Principatelor Unite 1859-1862*, The Institute of Historic Studies and Researches, Iasi, 1959.
- Anastasiu, Ion, *Oastea romana de-a lungul veacurilor*, Bucharest, The Military Publishing House, 1972.
- Balcescu, Nicolae, *Romanii sup Mihai Voievod Viteazul*, edited by Andrei Rusu, Bucharest, 1982.
- Berindei, Dan, *Epoca Unirii*, Bucharest, 1979.
- Berindei, Dan, *L'Union des principautes Roumaines*, Bucharest, 1967.
- Berindei, Dan, *L'annee revolutionnaire de 1821 dans les Pays roumains*, Bucharest, 1971.
- *Bibliografia militara romaneasca* (1831-1983), vol. 1-4, Bucharest, 1975-1984.
- Barladeanu, Nicolae; Nicolaescu, Dan, *Contributii la istoria marinei romane, vol. I, Din cele mai vechi timpuri pana in 1918*, Bucharest, 1967.

- Bodea, Cornelia, *Lupta romanilor pentru unitate nationala* (1834-1849), Bucharest, 1967.
- Bolintineanu, Dimitrie, *Cuza Voda si oamenii sai. Memoriu istoric*, Bucharest, 1870.
- Brezoianu, Ion, *Reformele Romaniei sau colectiune de toate legile si regulamentele introduse in administratiunea romana*, 1859-1864, Bucharest, 1864.
- Cazanisteanu, Constantin; Cucu Mihai; Popescu, E., *Aspecte militare ale Revolutiei din 1848 in Tara Romaneasca*, Bucharest, 1968.
- Cazanisteanu, Constantin, *Probleme militare in revolutia de la 1848*, Bucharest, 1974.
- Chitu, I., *Evolutia institutiei si a tacticii infanteriei romanesti de la 1830 la 1931*, in "*Revista Infanteriei*," 1931.
- Ciuchi, Il, (Lieutenant-Commander), *Istoria marinei romane in curs de secole*, 1906.
- Cliveti, Gheorghe, *Romania in conflictul franco-german (1870-1871),* in "AHAI," 2, pages 157-180.
- Cristea, Gheorghe, *La guerre franco-allemande et le mouvement republicain de mars 1871 a Bucarest*, in "RRH" 9, 1974, 2, pages 277-291.

Bibliography

- Constantinescu, Ioan, *Indicator general al tuturor legilor si regulamentelor decretate si publicate in Monitorul Oficial de la anul 1860 pana la 30 March 1897*, Bucharest, 1997.
- Costescu, Dimitrie, *Fazele ministeriale in Romania (1862-1936),* Bucharest, 1936.
- Cristache, Gheorghe, *Formatiuni populare militare romanesti (1800-1830),* Bucharest, The Military Publishing House, 1982.
- Crutescu, Radu, *Amintirile colonelului Lacusteanu*, Bucharest, 1935.
- Damean, Sorin-Liviu, *Carol I al Romaniei. Profilul omului de stat*, in "Omagiu istoricului Gheorghe Buzatu," Focsani, 1999, pages 172-193.
- Dumitrescu, Al., *Contributii la istoricul armei artileriei*, in "Revista artileriei," Bucharest, XLI, no. 7-8, 1934.
- Dumitrescu, Mihail, *Amintiri si episoade din razboiul de independenta*, Bucharest, 1893-
- *Elemente de strategie militara*, Bucharest, 1975.
- Emerit, Marcel, *Une ingerence francaise dans la politique interieure roumaine au debut du regne de Carol Ier*, in "RHSEE," 16, 1939, pages 53-73.
- *File din istoria militara a poporului roman: Studii*, Bucharst, 1982.

- Filitti, I.C., *Domniile romane sub Regulamentul Organic*, Bucharest, 1915.
- Florescu, Radu R., *The Struggle against Russia in the Romanian Principalities*, Munich, 1961 (reprinted in 1998).
- Gane, N., *P.P. Carp si rolul sau in istoria politica a tarii*, 1, Bucharest, 1936.
- Georgescu, D. I., *Istoria armatei romane si a razboaielor poporului roman*, Bucharest, 1929.
- Georgescu, Maria, *Cadeti romani la Saint Cyr*, Bucharest, 2002.
- Georgescu, Maria, *Politica militara a guvernarii liberale din anii 1867-1868*, in "File din istoria militara a poporului roman," 3, 1975, pages 120-138.
- Georgescu, Maria et Cpt. Christophe Midan, *Un exemple de cooperation bilaterale. Les attaches militaries francais en Roumanie et roumains en France 1840-1940*, Bucharest, 2003.
- Giurescu, Constantin C., *Viata si opera lui Cuza*, Bucharest, 1966.
- Hamangiu, Constantin, *Cadrul general al Romaniei*, Bucharest, 1900.
- Hentea, Calin, *Armata si luptele romanilor*, Bucharest, 2002.
- *Istoria gandirii militare romanesti*, Bucharest, 1974.
- Iorga, Nicolae, *Istoria lui Mihai Viteazul*, Bucharest, 1968.

Bibliography

- Iorga, Nicolae, *Istoria armatei romanesti*, Bucharest, 1970.
- Iorga, Nicolae, *Politica externa a regelui Carol I*, Bucharest, 1923.
- *Istoria artileriei romane*, Bucharest, 1977.
- *Istoria militara a poporului roman, vol. I, Din cele mai vechi timpuri pana in secolul al XIV-lea*, Bucharest, 1864, page 16.
- Kogalniceanu, Mihail, *Cuvant asupra proiectului de organizare militara*, Bucharest, 1864, 16.
- Lahovary, George Ioan, *Hartii vechi. Geneza ostirei romane (1830),* Bucharest, 1893.
- Lindenberg, Paul, *Konig Karl von Rumanien*, vol. 1-2, Berlin, 1923.
- Logofatu, Gheorghe (General-Lieutenant), *Elemente de strategie militara*, Bucharest, 1975.
- Lungu, P. Traian, *Viata politica in romania la sfarsitul secolului at XIX-lea (1888-1899)*, Bucharest, 1967.
- Michelson, Paul E., *Conflict and Crisis: Romanian Political Development, 1861-1871*, New York, 1987.
- Nadejde, V. (Lieutenant-Colonel), *Centenarul renasterii armatei romane, 1830-1930*, Bucharest.
- Neagoe, Stelian, *Istoria guvernelor Romaniei de la inceputuri – 1859 – pana in zilele noastre – 1995*, Bucharest, 1995.

- Neagoe, Stelian, *Un martor ocular. Memoriile Regelui Carol al Romaniei*, Bucharest, 1995.
- Niculescu, Gheorghe, *Parlamentul roman. Scurta expunere in ordine cronologica a regimului nostru parlamentar de la 1866 pana astazi*, Bucharest, 1903.
- Otetea, Andrei, *Tudor Vladimirescu si revolutia din 1821*, Bucharest, 1971.
- *Pagini din gandirea militara romaneasca*, Collection of texts, Bucharest, 1969.
- *Pagini din istoria pompierilor. Contributia pompierilor militari la lupta pentru libertate sociala si nationala a poporului roman (1835-1878),* Bucharest, 1976.
- Pencovici, Eustatiu (General), *Recrutarea – explicarea legei. Introducere. Modeluri. Circulare*, Bucharest, 1862.
- Popa, Anghel, *Renasterea armatei pamantene in Moldova, Campulung, 1955.*
- Popa, Anghel, *Istoria artileriei romane*, Bucharest, 1977.
- Popescu, Nicolai D., *Istoria resbelului romano-ruso-turc 1875-1878*. Bucharest, 1889.
- Popovici, Ioan (Major), *Organizarea armatei romane. Schita istorica a organizarii, 1830-1877*, vol. I., Bucharest, 1900.

Bibliography

- *Reformele Romanilor sau colectiune de toate legile si regulamentele introduse in administratia Romaniei de la 1859 ianuarie pana la 1864 octombrie*, Bucharest, 1864.
- Riker, T. W., *Cums s-a infaptuit Romania (The Making of Romania),* Bucharest, 1944.
- Romanescu, Gheorghe, *Oastea romana de-a lungul veacurilor*, Bucharest, 1976.
- *Romanii de la 1859. Unirea Principatelor in constiinta europeana*, vol. 1, 2, Bucharest, 1984.
- Rosetti, Radu R., *Istoria artei militare a romanilor pana la mijlocul veacului at XVII-lea*, Bucharest, 1947.
- Rosetti, Radu R., *Artileria in trecutul romanesc*, Pitesti, 1943.
- Rosetti, Radu R., *Partea luata de armata romana in razboiul din 1877-1878*, Bucharest, 1926.
- *Decoratii romanesti de Razboi 1860-1947*, Bucharest.
- Savu, Al., *Pages de l'histoire de l'armee roumaine*, Bucharest, 1976.
- Serbanescu, Horia V. L., and Co., *Armata romana in Razboiul de Independenta 1877-1878*, Bucharest, 1992.
- Soare, Corneliu (General), *Istoria gandirii militare romanesti*, Bucharest, 1974.

- Stefanescu, Gerorge, *Indicator general, cuprinzand legile, regulamentele, inaltele decrete, deciziuni, ordine circulare si diferite instructii militare si date publicate prin Monitorul Oficial si Monitorul Oastei de la anul 1860 pana la l Ianuarie 1890 de Administratorul clasa II din Ministerul de Razboi*, Bucharest, 1890.
- Totu, Maria, *Garda civila din Romania 1848-1884*, Bucharest, 1976.
- Vasilescu, Gerorge, *Repertoriul legilor, decretelor regale, jurnalelor, consiliilor de ministri si deciziunilor ministeriale uzuale (1862-1935),* Bucharest, 1935.
- Vladescu, Cristian M., *Uniformele armatei romane (incep. Sec. XIX – mai 1945),* Bucharest, 1977

SPECIAL WORKS, STUDIES AND ARTICLES

- Angelescu, Constantin, *Dezvoltarea constitutionala a principatelor Unite de la 1859-1862*, in "Studii si cercetari stiintifice," Iasi, History, Year X, 1959, no. 1-2, pages 151-174.
- Batalli, Ion, *Armamentul din dotarea armatei romane in timpul Razboiului de Independenta*, in "Studii si materiale de muzeografie si istorie militara," Central Military Museum, Bucharest, year II, no. 2-3, 1969-1970, pages 158-171.
- Batalli, Ion, *Generalul Ioan Emanoil Florescu, un precursor al armatei romane moderne*, in "Studii si materiale de muzeografie si istorie militara," Central Military Museum, Bucharest, no. 9, 1976, pages 75-78.
- Berindei, Dan, *Guvernele lui Alexandru Ioan Cuza. Lista de ministrere,* in "Revista Arhivelor," 1959, no. 1., pages 147-163.
- Bodea, Cornelia, si Cernovodeanu, Paul, *Primele scoli ostasesti din Tara Romaneasca (1838-1840)*, in "Studii si aricole de istorie," VII Bucharest, 1966, pages 105-116.
- Cazanisteanu, Constantin; Gheorghe, Tudor, *Armata româna în preajma Razboiului de Independenta 1877-1878*, in the

volume "Romania in Razboiul de Independenta 1877-1878," Bucharest, The Military Publishing House, 1977.

- Cazanisteanu, Constantin, *Primele arme romanesti fabricate la manufactura din bucuresti (1865),* "Studies and Materials of Museography and Military History," Central Military Museum, no. 2-3, 1969-1970, pages 277-280.
- Craciunariu, Serban, *Din preocuparile domnitorului Alexandru Ioan Cuza pentru sporirea efectivelor armate in 1859* in "Analele Universitatii Craiova" I, 1972, pages 68-75.
- Dumitrescu, Al., *Contributiuni la istoricul armei artileriei*, in "Revista Artileriei," Bucharest, 1934.
- Emerit, Marcel, *Une conversation entre l'empereur Napoleon III et Basil Alecsandri*, in "Revue historique du Sud Est Europen," no. 7-9, 1928, pages 232-236.
- Emerit, Marcel, *Le dossier de la premiere mission militaire francaise en Roumanie (1860-1866),* in "Revue roumaine d'histoire," no. 4, 1966, pages 575-586.
- Fetcu, Ioan, *Armata romana in timpul domniei lui Alexandru Ioan Cuza (1859-1866),* "Studii si materiale de muzeografie si istorie militara," Central Military Museum, no. 7-8, 1974-1975.

Bibliography

- Florescu, Radu R., *Dumitru Florescu: A Forgotten Pioneer in the History of Romanian Music,* "Unirea," Bucharest, 1984.
- Florescu, Radu R., *Elena Cuza dincolo de legenda,* "Magazin Istoric," 1988, June.
- Florescu, Radu R., *Creatorul armatei romane moderne,* "Magazin Istoric," 1993, June.
- Florescu, Radu R., *Hora lul Cuza,* "Magazin Istoric", 1986, January.
- Georgescu, Maria, *Misiunea militara franceza in Romania 1869-1869,* The Institute for Political Studies of Defense and Military History, Bucharest, 1997.
- Konig, Carol; Vladescu M., Cristian, *Armamentul armatei romane in razboiul pentru obtinerea lndependentei de Stat a Romaniei din 1877-1878,* in "Studii si materiale de muzeografie si istorie militara," Central Military Museum, no.10, 1977, pages 151-186.
- Konig, Carol, *Un manuscris valoros in cunoasterea evolutiei armamentului si munitiei in dotarea armatei romane, aflat in colectia Muzeului Militar Central,* in "Studii si materiale de muzeografie si istorie militara," Central Military Museum, no. 10, 1977, pages 287-292.

- Nasturel, p. V., *Contributii la istoria artileriei romane*, "Revista Artileriei," July-August, 1906.
- Palanceanu, Elena, *Cu privire la masurile luate de Alexandru Ioan Cuza in anii 1859-1861 pentru unificarea si organizarea armatei* in "Studii si materiale de museografie si istorie militara," Central Military Museum, no. 4-5, 1971, pages 126-141.
- Popescu, Teodor, *Gandirea social-politica despre inarmarea maselor oglindita in presa civila, dezbaterile parlamentare si legislatia militara din timpul domniei lui Alexandru Ioan Cuza*, in "File din istoria militara a poporului roman," Studies, volume I, The Military Publishing House
- Radovici, Maria, *Pagini din istoricul publicatiilor militare (1859-1916),* in "Studii si materiale de muzeografie si istorie militara," Central Military Museum, no. 2-3, 1969-1970, pages 146-157.
- Radovici, Maria, *Ajutorul acordat Serbiei in 1876 de catre ambulanta, "Societatii Crucea rosie din Romania,"* in "Studii si materiale de muzeografie si istorie militara," Central Military Museum, no. 9, 1976, pages 79-88.

Bibliography

- Scates, Cornel, *Din istoricul dotarii armatei romane*, in "Studii si materiale de muzeografie si istorie militara," Central Military Museum, no. 10, 1977, pages 187-196.
- Stan, Maria, *Contributii la cunoaasterea invatamantului militar, in secolul al XIX-lea*, in "Studii si materiale de muzeografie si istorie military," Central Military Museum, no. 6, 1973, pages 128-135.
- Tarnoviceanu, I., *Pagini din domnia lui Cuza-Voda*, in "Revista pentru istorie, arheologie, filologie," vol. XIII, page 23.
- Vladescu, M. Cristian, *Harnasamentul armatei române, model 1872 folosit in razboiul pentru obtinerea independentei de stat a Romaniei*, in "Studii si materiale do muzeografie si istorie military," Central Miitary Museum, no. 10, 1977, pages 143-150.
- Vladescu, M., Cristian, *Contributii la cunoasterea uniformelor de cavalerie din perioada lui Al, Ioan Cuza (1859-1866),* in "Studii si materiale de muzeografie si istorie militara," Central Military Museum, 1968, pages 197-212.

WORKS ON GENERAL I. E. FLORESCU

- *I. EM. Florescu general de divizie*, "Schita istorica," Bucharest, 1877.
- *Generalul I. Em. Florescu (1819-1893)*, Bucharest, 1908. (Author unknown).
- Ionnescu-Gion, g. I., *Din istoria contemporana a romanilor. Generalul Florescu*, Bucharest, 1894.
- Rosetti, Radu (General), *Un uitat: Generalul Ioan Emanoil Florescu*, Bucharest, 1937.
- Rosetti, Radu, (General), *Partea luata de armata romana in razboiul din 1877-1878*, Bucharest, 1926.
- Rosetti, Radu, (General), *Corespondenta generalului Grigore Cantilli*, Bucharest, n.d.
- Batalli, Ion, *Generalul Ioan Emanoil Florescu, un precursor al armatei romane moderne*, in "Studii si materiale de muzeografie si istorie military," Central Military Museum, Bucharest, no. 9, 1977.
- Radu R. Florescu, *General Ioan Emanoil Florescu, Father of the Romanian Army in War and Society in East Central Europe*, New York 1985.

Bibliography

- Florescu, Radu, R., *Cuza – Florescu and Army Reform, in War and Society in East Central Europe*, New York, 1985.
- Florescu, Radu, R., *Florescu si reforma armatei 1859-1866*, in "Din istoria militara a poporului roman," vol. XII, Bucharest, 1984.

WORKS BY GENERAL IOAN EMANOIL FLORESCU

Bibliographic Chronology

- *Cinci schite de copii care au ajuns oameni de seama*, in "Muzeul Nattional," no. 39 of December, 1836.
- *Teoria darii la semn*, printed by Zaharia Carcalechi, printer of the Court, Bucharest, 1845.
- *Romania*, "legi si decrete," Iasi, 1859.
- *Romania, "Regulamentele militare*," Bucharest, n.d.
- *Espunere de imbunatatirile cele mai insemnatoare introduse in armata Principatelor Unite de la 24 ianuarie 1859-1 iunie 1861*, Bucharest, 1861.
- *Inalta ordonanta din 21 August (1862) asupra serviciului armatei in campanie*, Bucharest, 1862.
- *Instructiuni extrase din Legea reorganizarii dorobantilor din 1850 si din alte dispozitii ulterioare (1864),* Bucharest, 1864.
- *Instructiuni extrase din Legea reorganizarii granicerilor, promulgata in 1850 si alte dispozitii ulterioare*, Bucharest, 1864.
- *Instructiuni extrase din Legea Organizarii granicerilor,* Bucharest, 1864.

Bibliography

- *Raspuns la referintele si brosurile Domnului Sturzda, ministrul actual de Lucrari Publice*, Bucharest, 1866.
- *Datoriile ostasului* (translation of the work of the French Captain Rocquancourt), Bucharest, 1876.
- *Discurs tinut in Senat cu ocazia votarii legii pentru contingentul armatei*
- *(March 12, 1877),* Bucharest, 1877.
- *Studii si pregatiri militare*, Bucharest, 1878.
- *Situatiunea*, Bucharest, 1878.
- *Institutiunea armatei bazata pe scoala*, Bucharest, 14 February 1885.
- *Cateva cuvinte asupra intrarii in actiune a trupelor noastre*, Bucharest, 1887.
- *Fortificatiunile* (a speech delivered in the Senate, session of May 7, 1889), Bucharest.
- *Discurs relativ la creditul cerut pentru fortificatii* (in the Senate session of May 4, 1890), Bucharest, 1890.
- *Osebirea intre armatele vechi si moderne*, a speech delivered on April 11, 1890, Bucharest, 1890.
- *Discursul cu ocazia pietrei fundamentale a Ateneului Roman*, Bucharest, n.d.